Pickles, Chutneys and Preserves

Over 150 Ways of Preserving Fruits and Vegetables

Other Books by the same Author

The Vegetarian Menu Book
The Complete Vegetable Cookbook

Pickles, Chutneys and Preserves

Over 150 Ways of Preserving Fruits and Vegetables

Vasantha Moorthy

 UBSPD

UBS Publishers' Distributors Ltd.

New Delhi ● Mumbai ● Bangalore ● Chennai

Calcutta ● Patna ● Kanpur ● London

UBS Publishers' Distributors Ltd.

5 Ansari Road, New Delhi-110 002
Phones: 3273601, 3266646 ● *Cable* : ALLBOOKS ● *Fax* : (91) 11-327-6593
E-mail: ubspd.del@smy.sprintrpg.ems.vsnl.net.in
Internet: www.ubspd.com
Apeejay Chambers, 5 Wallace Street, Mumbai-400 001
Phones : 2076971, 2077700 ● *Cable* : UBSIPUB ● *Fax* : 2070827
10 First Main Road, Gandhi Nagar, Bangalore-560 009
Phones : 2263901, 2263902, 2253903 ● *Cable* : ALLBOOKS ● *Fax* : 2263904
6, Sivaganga Road, Nungambakkam, Chennai-600 034
Phone : 8276355, 8270189 ● *Cable* : UBSIPUB ● *Fax* : 8278920
8/1-B, Chowringhee Lane, Calcutta-700 016
Phones : 2441821, 2442910, 2449473 ● *Cable* : UBSIPUBS ● *Fax* : 2450027
5 A, Rajendra Nagar, Patna-800 016
Phones : 672856, 673973, 656170 ● *Cable* : UBSPUB ● *Fax* : 656169
80, Noronha Road, Cantonment, Kanpur-208 004
Phones : 369124, 362665, 357488 ● *Fax* : 315122

Overseas Contact:
475, North Circular Road, Neasden, London NW2 7QG
Tele: 0181-450-8667 ● *Fax*: 0181-452-6612 *Attn*: UBS

© Vasantha Moorthy

First Published 1999

Cover design : Ilaksha
Photographs : T. S. Satyan

Printed at Pauls Press, New Delhi

To my husband for his unwavering encouragement and to
my son, Girish, for his tireless efforts in bringing out my cookbooks

Acknowledgements

I am extremely grateful to Ranga and Karthik who undertook the difficult task of converting my hand-written papers into the form you see today. Next, I thank Gautam, Shiela and Vivek for their individual contributions in putting the finishing touches to the manuscript. I also appreciate the efforts of D.V.S. Murthy in compiling the index, and those of Eileen Winchell who proofread the drafts and made many helpful suggestions.

TABLE OF CONTENTS

INTRODUCTION

Vegetables and fruits are seasonal and perishable. Hence the need to preserve them in the form of pickle, chutney, jam and squash. These preserves have a delectable taste of their own and supplement the daily menu.

In our country, pickles and chutneys have always been a part of the cuisine and hence we have a wide variety and range of these from different regions. In this book I have compiled over 150 recipes not only from various parts of our country but also from different parts of the world. The reader has a choice of either trying her hand at her grandmother's cherished recipe or attempting something new from other regions or countries. At a glance, she can choose pickle or chutney, jam or squash, according to her needs, and stock her larder with a whole range of products. As I have done in my second book, *The Complete Vegetable Cookbook* (UBSPD), I have indicated, wherever possible, the region or the state to which the recipe belongs.

To make it easier and to familiarise her with the process of preservation, I have given "Basic Notes" in the following pages which will be useful. A glossary for some of their ingredients has also been included.

The hints on making jam, jelly, marmalade and squash as well as the table for various fruits for making squash have been compiled from notes taken during demonstration classes by the Food and Nutrition Department of Mumbai, Home Science College, Bangalore and the Canning Centre, Guwahati. A few recipes have been taken from my earlier books, *The Vegetarian Menu Book*, and *The Complete Vegetable Cookbook*, as they are relevant to this book.

I am sure you will enjoy making these recipes and find them economical too. I wish you all success in this venture.

Bangalore   **VASANTHA MOORTHY**

Basic Rules for the Preparation of Jam, Jelly and Marmalade

1. The general method of preparation is common to all fruit jams. Always select firm, ripe but not overripe fruits. Wash them thoroughly in cold water, carefully and gently removing dust and dirt.

2. Use a sharp, stainless steel knife to cut and chop fruits.

3. Use a large heavy-bottomed pan to cook the jam or jelly so as to allow sufficient room for boiling without boiling over. A pressure cooker could serve the purpose. Use wooden ladles or spoons for cooking.

4. Rub the bottom of pan with a little butter to prevent the jam from sticking, before adding fruit and water.

5. Simmer the fruit until tender . The skin of the fruit should be soft before adding sugar, as sugar tends to harden the skin.

6. Follow the recipe for the exact amount of sugar and citric acid. Citric acid is not only used for flavour but since it also prevents recrystallisation of sugar, it must be added to the jam even when the fruit is sour. If you are making a very small quantity, then lime juice will suffice.

7. For 1 cup of fruit pulp use 3/4 cup sugar. Sugar may be increased if the fruit is very sour. As a general rule, use 1/4 teaspoon of citric acid for 1 cup pulp, but decrease it to a pinch in the case of sour fruits. Add the colour and essence to taste.

8. After adding sugar to the fruit, stir constantly until sugar has dissolved completely so that the product does not burn during cooking.

9. Once the sugar has dissolved, allow the jam to boil rapidly without stirring so that it sets more quickly.

10. Test for setting. After sufficient boiling, when the mixture has reached jam consistency, test as follows: a drop put on a ceramic plate does not spread. When this consistency is reached take a little jam in a teaspoon, cool and drop this into a bowl of water. If the drop settles at the bottom without disintegrating it shows that the sugar has reached 70% concentration which is **absolutely necessary** as

this is the only method of **preservation**. A little more will make it sticky and hard. While testing remove pan from fire and, if necessary, return it to the fire to achieve the correct concentration.

11. When test shows jam consistency, remove from fire, add the colour and essence (optional) drop by drop. Mix thoroughly, then pour the hot jam into sterilised bottles, seal and store.

12. For extra care in the preservation of jam, 1/4 teaspoon of Sodium Benzoate can be added for every 1 kg of pulp.

Preparation of Jelly

1. Jelly is prepared from fruits rich in pectin which is a must for jelly to set. Apples, guavas, pineapples, strawberries, raspberries and currants are rich in pectin. For apple and guava jelly select a mixture of raw and ripe fruit - 2 raw and 1 ripe fruit. While raw fruit yields pectin, ripe fruit gives the colour and flavour to jelly.

2. Wash and chop the fruits. **Do not peel** as the peel contains pectin. Add enough water to cover the fruits, half the quantity of citric acid and cook for 20 to 30 minutes until soft and mushy.

3. Strain the fruit through a thin muslin cloth or jelly bag. **Do not squeeze**, as it will cloud the end product. Allow the extract to fall in drops, overnight if possible, since this procedure takes time.

4. Add the sugar and the rest of the citric acid to the strained liquid and boil, stirring all the while until the sugar dissolves.

5. Once the sugar has dissolved, **do not stir**, but allow to boil briskly (by raising the heat) for one to two minutes. Remove and strain once again.

6. To the strained juice add the colour and essence, and cook further until the mixture falls in flakes.

7. Test for setting. Stir the wooden spoon thoroughly, so it coats fully. Allow to cool, then lift spoon horizontally and allow the jelly to drop on a plate. If the drop falls immediately it is not yet set. But if the drop holds on to the spoon and falls like a 'flake' or sheet, it has reached the setting point. This is also referred to as **sheet consistency**. While testing remove pan from fire, and if it is not set, return pan to the fire, and repeat this process until the correct consistency is reached.

8. When the jelly has set, pour into sterilised jars and seal.

Note: For every 600 ml of juice allow 450 gm sugar, or for 1 pint juice use 1 lb sugar.

Preparation of Marmalade

1. The preparation and proportion of ingredients is the same as for jelly. The difference is in the taste. Marmalade has a bitter-sweet taste due to the presence of shreds of citrus peel. Marmalade is a combination of fruits like oranges and lemons, apples and oranges, guavas and sweet lime along with the peels.

2. Citrus fruit should be peeled and the pulp used for pectin extract. After peeling scrape the inside white portion thoroughly, discard this; then cut the peel into fine shreds. For fruits like guavas and apples the fruits are used without peeling.

3. Boil the shreds in water, changing the water two to three times until the peels turn very soft. Tie them in a spice bag or a thin, white muslin cloth and add to pan when the pulp and sugar are boiling.

4. When the syrup reaches a sheet consistency the jelly will fall in flakes. Remove bag, open it and put the shreds at the bottom of the sterilised bottles.

5. Pour the hot syrup on top, so that the shreds are distributed. Leave the bottles open to cool and then seal.

Preparation of Squash

Squashes are prepared from juicy fruits like oranges, lemons, sweet limes (musambi), grapes, pineapples, and both raw and ripe mangoes. The method of preparation is common to all fruits except in the proportion of sugar and citric acid used.

General Method of Preparation

1. Choose only ripe, juicy fruits without any spots or blemishes. Wash thoroughly and extract juice manually or with an electric juicer.

2. For hard pulp fruits like pineapple and raw mango, peel and cut the fruit into pieces, adding just enough water. Boil until soft, cool, and strain to extract the juice. For ripe mango, peel the fruit and squeeze gently to extract the juice.

3. Measure the juice and take sugar, water and citric acid in the proper proportions according to the table below. Set aside the juice.

4. Add water to the sugar, and boil until it dissolves. Add the citric acid and boil further to form a syrup. Remove from fire, strain through a thin cloth to remove the scum. For lemon squash 1 teaspoon of lime juice is added to syrup instead of citric acid.

5. Cool the syrup thoroughly and then add the juice, otherwise the juice will curdle. Add the colour and essence to taste.

6. Lastly add the preservative before bottling.

7. Refer to the table below for making squashes with different types of fruits.

Table for Making Squash

	FRUIT	JUICE	SUGAR	WATER	CITRIC ACID
1.	Lemon and Raw Mango	1 cup	2 1/2 cups	1 cup	1 tsp of juice for lemon squash, 1/4 tsp citric acid for raw mango
2.	Pineapple and pome-granate	1 cup	1 3/4 cup	1 3/4 cup	1/2 tsp
3.	Orange, sweet lemon or grape	1 cup	1 1/4 cup	3/4 cup	3/4 tsp
4.	Ripe mango	1 cup	1 cup	1 cup	1 tsp

Approximate Conversions

1 oz.	=	28 gm		
1oz.	=	2 tablespoons		
1 tablespoon	=	4 teaspoons		
1 teacup (standard)	=	5 oz.	=	50 cc
1 standard tumbler	=	8 oz.	=	1/2 pint
1 pint	=	600 ml	=	2 1/2 cups
1 lb	=	0.454 kg		

Solid Measurement

4 oz.   =   100 gm = 1 cup

A Word on Preservation

Fruit products like jam, jelly, preserves, marmalade, and syrup are preserved by having greater than a 70% concentration of sugar in them. But there are other products like squash, sauce, chutney and ketchup which contain little or no sugar. Here the products are preserved by the addition of:

KMS - Potassium Meta Bisulphate or
NAB - Sodium Benzoate.

For light colour products use KMS and for dark colour products NAB is preferred.

Proportion of preservative to be used

For 1 litre of finished product, use 1/8 teaspoon of KMS or 1/4 teaspoon of NAB. As mentioned earlier, citric acid is not used as a preservative but to enhance the flavour of the product, to remove dirt or scum in the sugar, and to prevent recrystallisation of sugar.

Note: If you do not wish to use preservatives, the product may not last as long as specified, and must be consumed quickly.

Bottling

1. Put washed, cleaned bottles in cold water and heat them along with the water. After it starts boiling allow the water to boil 5 minutes more, then remove bottles from water and keep them upside down on a wooden plank for a few minutes. You may even dry them in the sun. Now they are sterilised.

2. Never wipe the bottles with cloth once they are sterilised.

3. Always sterilise the bottles only on the day you are going to use them, never earlier.

4. Always use wide-mouthed bottles, the capacity of the bottle being equal to the content of jam you are making. This is because the jam has to be filled **to the brim,** to remove any air present in the bottle. There should be a head space of two to three inches for squashes.

5. In the case of jam/jelly pour while it is still hot into hot, sterilised bottles. Leave bottles open to cool before sealing. For squashes, the products should be thoroughly cooled before bottling.

Sealing

1. Melt 2 teaspoons of wax, and pour on top of jam which will spread and form a seal making it air tight. Then cover the bottles or use a tight-fitting lid.

2. Store products in cool, dark places. Once sealed, the product should last for some time. Once the seal is broken, refrigerate and consume quickly.

General Hints on Pickles and Chutneys

1 . Fruits and vegetables used for pickles and chutneys should be very fresh, firm and without blemish. They should be washed thoroughly and if necessary wiped with a clean cloth before use. Traces of water will make the pickle rancid.

2. Masalas should be very fresh, especially powdered ones. Get the masalas ready the same day or a day before you get the vegetables.

3. If you are making mango pickle, the mangoes should be hard with the seeds having formed, unless specified otherwise.

4. Use stainless steel, enamel or earthenware jars for mixing. **Do not use aluminium or brass.**

5. Use a sharp, stainless steel knife for cutting and chopping.

6. Always store pickles in earthenware jars or glass bottles. Cover the mouth of the jar with a clean muslin cloth.

7. See that there is oil on the surface of the pickle. Otherwise it will spoil. Oil acts as a preservative.

8. When you are making pickles to last a year, **sun** them, either as pieces before pickling, or when ready, keep the pickle in the sun for a few days before storing.

9. When you are making vegetable pickle which requires cooking, see that it is thoroughly cooled before bottling.

10. Before using salt, it can be broiled (dry roasted) on a low flame for a couple of minutes. This removes the moisture in the salt which helps preservation.

11. In the Western method of preparation of pickles and chutneys, where vinegar is used, use only a part of it in the beginning, and the rest while cooking or at the end.

12. Always use vinegar for grinding dry masalas for chutney or pickle.

13. Cook chutney in an open pan without the lid and stir constantly.

14. As in the case of jams pour chutney up to the brim while it is still hot.

15. Follow the recipe for sugar and vinegar - do not reduce the amount as both of them act as preservatives.

16. Before storing see that the vinegar covers the surface of vegetables, especially in the case of tomato sauce.

APPLE

1. **Apple Jam**

2. **Apple Jelly**

3. **Apple Orange Marmalade**

4. **Apple Carrot Jam (Indian)**

5. **Apple Chutney (Indian)**

6. **Apple Relish (Western)**

7. **Apple Tomato Chutney (Western)**

8. **Apple Juice (Western)**

Apple Jam

Ingredients

apples (sour variety)
sugar
citric acid
a few drops of red food colour

Method

1. Wash, peel, core and grate the apples. Weigh the gratings. For every 1 kg of gratings, use 1 kg sugar and 1 teaspoon of citric acid. Keep separate.

2. To the apple gratings add some water and simmer gently until thick and mushy.

3. Add sugar and citric acid, and continue to cook gently until sugar has dissolved, stirring all the time.

4. When all the sugar has dissolved, raise the heat and allow the jam to boil so as to reach setting point quickly (do not stir). If set quickly the jam will have a better flavour and colour. Test for setting. Refer to the hints on jam making at the beginning of the book.

5. When set remove from fire, add the colour and mix thoroughly. Pour into sterilised bottles and seal.

Apple Ginger Jam
(a variation of apple jam)

The ingredients are the same except for the addition of ginger in step 2.
In step 2, add 1 teaspoon of ground ginger to the pulp when cooking.
In step 5, when set, add 1 teaspoon of fine slivers of crystallised ginger along with the colour.

Apple Jelly

Ingredients

1 1/2 kg cooking apples
5 cups boiling water
juice of 1 large lemon
sugar

Method

1. Wash, wipe and chop the apples. Do not peel or core. Add water and simmer slowly until fruit is soft and mushy.

2. Remove from fire, and transfer the pulp to a jelly bag (or use a thin muslin cloth tied loosely).

3. Suspend bag over a bowl and allow the juice to drip, overnight if possible, as it takes a long time.

4. Measure the juice - to every 600 ml of juice (extract) add 450 grams of sugar. Mix both together, add the lemon juice and boil briskly until set. Refer to the general hints on jelly at the beginning of this book.

5. Remove from fire, pour into sterilised jars and seal.

Apple Mint Jelly
(a variation of apple jelly)

If you desire a fresh minty flavour add 1-1 1/2 teaspoons of finely minced mint leaves in step 4, either directly or tied in a spice bag. You could add a few drops of green colour if desired.

Apple Orange Marmalade

Ingredients

    1/2 kg cooking apples
    1/2 kg orange peel
    1 1/2 kg sugar
    6 cups water

Method

1. Use a sufficient number of oranges to yield 1/2 kg of peel. Wash and peel the oranges. Scrape the white portion on the inside of the peel. Discard this. Wash thoroughly and cut peel into fine shreds. Soak shreds in water overnight; next day simmer shreds gently until soft.

2. Wash, peel and chop the apples. Add to the orange peel while it is cooking; cook fruit to a smooth pulp.

3. Add the sugar and boil without stirring until the mixture reaches setting point. Refer to the general hints on marmalade at the beginning of this book.

4. Pour into sterilised jars and seal.

Apple Carrot Jam (Indian)
(with ginger flavour)

Ingredients

    1/4 kg firm apples (cooking variety)
    150 gm carrots
    1 small piece of fresh ginger (minced)
    juice of 1 small lemon
    350 gm sugar
    a pinch of cinnamon powder
    a few drops of orange food colour (optional)

Method

1. Wash, peel and grate the apples and carrots.

2. Put these into a thick bottomed sauce pan. Add the minced ginger, lemon juice and sugar. Cook on low heat until the sugar has dissolved.

3. Raise the heat and cook further until a jam consistency is reached. Test for setting. Refer to the general hints on jam making at the beginning of this book.

4. Remove from fire, add the cinnamon powder and colour. Mix thoroughly. Pour into sterilised bottles and seal.

Apple Chutney (Indian)

Ingredients

1 kg apples (cooking variety)
2-3 cups sugar, depending on tartness of apples
250 gm onions
150 gm ginger
100 gm garlic
15 gm dried red chillies
or 3 teaspoons chilly powder
2 cups vinegar
40 gm salt

Method

1. Clean and grate the apples. Chop the onions, ginger and garlic. Pound the red chillies.

2. Add the chopped ingredients, chilly powder and 1 cup of vinegar to the grated apples and cook until the apples and onions have become soft and the mixture is almost dry.

3. Now add the sugar, salt and the other cup of vinegar. Cook further until the mixture is of a chutney consistency.

4. Remove from fire, cool and bottle.

Apple Relish (Western)

Ingredients   **Tie in a spice bag**

1/2 kg cooking apples   1/2 tsp ginger paste
1/4 kg onions   2 cloves
1/4-1/2 cup raisins   1 large cardamom
1/2 cup vinegar   1/2" stick cinnamon
1 1/2 cups sugar   1/2 tsp minced garlic (optional)
1/2 tsp salt

Method

1. Mince or grate the onions. Peel and chop the apples.

2. Put these into a thick-bottomed saucepan, add the spice bag, 1/4 cup vinegar, raisins and cook gently stirring occasionally until the fruit is soft.

3. Add the sugar, the rest of the vinegar and boil steadily until it reaches a chutney consistency.

4. Discard spice bag after squeezing all the liquid from the bag. Pour the relish into hot jars and seal.

Apple Tomato Chutney (Western)

Ingredients	**Tie in a spice bag**
1/2 kg sour apples	2-3 cloves
150 gm tomatoes	1/2" stick cinnamon
1 medium onion	2 large cardamoms
45 gm raisins	1 /2 tsp chilly powder
50 gm brown sugar	1/4 tsp pepper
3/4 cup vinegar	
salt to taste	

Method

1. Wash, peel and chop the apples and onions. Wash and chop the tomatoes. Put all together in a saucepan.

2. To this add the spice bag, raisins, sugar, salt and vinegar. Simmer until it reaches a chutney consistency. Remove from fire. Discard the spice bag after squeezing all the liquid in the bag. Pour the chutney into hot sterilised jars and seal.

Apple Juice (Western)

Ingredients

1/4 kg apples
1 cup water
1 small lemon
sugar to taste

Method

1. Wash and chop the apples.

2. Wash and peel the lemon. Scrape the inside white portion of the lemon, discard and then cut the peel into fine shreds. Set the lemon juice aside.

3. Put both the apples and peel together into a vessel with a tight-fitting lid.

4. Boil the water, pour over the apples, cover and allow to cool. When cold, strain. Add the sugar and lemon juice to taste.

Note

Chill and serve this juice immediately. *This is not to be preserved.*

If desired 1 teaspoon of mint leaves, chopped fine can be added in step 3.

APRICOT

1. **Apricot Jam (Fresh Fruit)**

2. **Apricot Jam (Dried Fruit)**

3. **Apricot Apple Chutney**

Apricot Jam (Fresh Fruit)

Ingredients

1/2 kg fresh apricots
1/2 kg sugar
1 1/4 cup water
juice of 1 lemon

Method

1. Wash and halve the apricots. Remove the stones. Break the stones, remove the kernels, and blanch them. (Put them in boiling water, and leave aside until the skin peels off.) Discard the water, peel the skin, dab the kernels on cloth or paper towels and when absolutely dry, cut into slivers (long thin pieces).

2. Chop fruit and add to pan along with the kernels. Add water and simmer till soft.

3. When the fruit has softened add the sugar and lemon juice, stirring all the while until the sugar has dissolved.

4. Now raise the heat and boil rapidly until the setting stage (12-15 minutes) is reached. Test for setting. Refer to the hints on jam making at the beginning of this book.

5. When set, remove from fire. Pour into warm sterilised jars and seal.

Apricot Jam (Dried Fruit)

Ingredients

1/2 kg dried apricots
1 1/2 kg sugar
7 1/2 - 8 cups water
juice of 2 small lemons
a few apricot kernels or almonds

Method

1. Wash and soak the apricots for 2 hours or until the fruit turns soft.

2. Extract juice of the lemons and grate the rind (after scraping off the white, inside portion of the skin).

3. Blanch and sliver the almonds or apricot kernels, as in step 1 of the previous recipe. Set aside.

4. Put the soaked apricots into a large pan, add the lemon juice and grated rind and simmer gently till fruit is tender.

5. Add the sugar and apricot kernels or almonds, and boil further until it sets. The jam here will not set very stiff but will have the consistency of thick syrup.

6. Pour the hot jam into sterilised jars and seal.

Apricot Apple Chutney

Ingredients

Spices

250 gm apples, peeled and grated
200 gm dried apricots
50 gm raisins
1/2 kg brown sugar
juice and peel of 1 lemon (small)
2 cloves of minced garlic (optional)
1/2" piece minced ginger
1 1/4 cups vinegar
salt to taste

1/2" cinnamon
2 cloves
2 cardamoms
5 peppercorns
1 red chilly broken

Method

1. Halve the apricots and remove the stones. Break the stones, remove the kernels, blanch in hot water, and cut into slivers. See the recipe for apricot jam (fresh fruit) for details. Set aside.

2. Chop the apricots, soak in water for 4-5 hours; drain all water. Put them into a cooking pan.

3. Add half the vinegar and all the other ingredients, except for the sugar and apples. Tie the spices in a bag, and add this to the pan. Simmer gently for about 30 minutes.

4. Now add the apples, sugar and the rest of the vinegar, and stir until the sugar has dissolved.

5. Boil mixture further until a thick chutney consistency is reached. Remove from fire.

6. Discard the spice bag, squeezing to remove any juice. Pour into hot jar and seal.

Note

This chutney can be prepared with apricots only. For this, omit the apples and use an additional 200 gm of apricots.

BANANA

---

1.   Banana Orange Lemon Jam

2.   Banana Softies

Banana Orange Lemon Jam

Ingredients

4 bananas
2 oranges
1 lemon
sugar

Method

1. Peel and cut the bananas into small pieces, and place in a pan.

2. Peel the oranges, extract the juice and strain. Add the pulp along with the juice to the bananas.

3. Scrape the inside white portion of the orange rind and grate. Add the gratings to the bananas. Extract juice of lemon, and add to pan.

4. Weigh the fruit pulp. For every 1 kg of pulp allow 3/4 kg sugar. Measure the sugar accordingly, sprinkle on fruit and allow to stand for 1-1 1/2 hours.

5. Place pan on flame, and bring it to a boil on very, very low heat. Boil till set. Refer to the hints on jam making at the beginning of this book. Pour into sterilised jars and seal.

Banana Softies

Ingredients

4 ripe bananas
1-1 1/2 cups sugar (to taste)
1 cup water
2 tbsp ghee
a large pinch of saffron (optional)
4 cardamoms (powdered)
1 tsp slivered almonds
a few almonds grated fine

Method

1. Soak the saffron in 1 teaspoon of hot water.

2. Mash the bananas along with sugar and add water. Mix thoroughly.

3. Place pan on very low fire, add the saffron and cook, stirring constantly until the sugar has dissolved.

4. Now raise the heat and cook briskly for 5-7 minutes stirring continuously.

5. Add the ghee and continue to cook until the mixture starts to leave the sides of the pan.

6. Remove from fire, add the cardamom and chopped almonds, and mix. Pour onto a greased plate, and spread evenly.

7. When cool, take out a small piece, make a ball, roll in the almond gratings and serve.

Note

You could serve this as halwa too. For this, follow this step. Remove pan from fire, add the cardamom and half the chopped almonds. Transfer to a serving bowl, even out the surface, and sprinkle the rest of the almonds on top.

BEETROOT

---

1. **Pickled Beetroot (Western)**

2. **Beetroot Chutney (Anglo-Indian)**

Pickled Beetroot (Western)

Ingredients

1/2 kg beetroot
salt to taste
spiced vinegar

For the spiced vinegar

2 1/2 cups vinegar (white)
3-4 cloves
half-inch piece ginger (minced)
a few peppercorns
2 half-inch pieces cinnamon
1 red chilly (broken)
2 black cardamoms
salt to taste

Method

1. Boil the beetroot, peel the skin, and cut into even-sized cubes. Set aside.

2. To 2 1/2 cups water add 1 teaspoon salt, and boil until it is dissolved. Add the beet cubes, and cook gently for 8-10 minutes.

3. Remove from fire, discard water completely and transfer to a pickle jar.

To prepare the spiced vinegar

1. Tie the spices loosely in a thin muslin cloth.

2. Pour the vinegar into a saucepan, add the salt and spice bag, and boil briskly for 12-15 minutes.

3. Remove from fire and squeeze the spice bag to remove all the liquid. Discard bag.

4. Pour enough hot spiced vinegar to cover the beet cubes fully, cover the mouth of the jar and leave in a cold place. Use after two to three days.

Note

You may prepare the spiced vinegar simultaneously while the beetroot is cooking.

Beetroot Chutney (Anglo-Indian)

Ingredients

500 gm beetroot (boiled, peeled and chopped)
200 gm apples (peeled, cored and chopped)
175 gm onions (peeled and chopped)
1 cup white vinegar, spiced (see above recipe for this)
2 tbsp raisins
2 tbsp sugar
salt to taste

Method

1. Put the onions into a saucepan, add a quarter cup vinegar, and cook on low heat until tender.

2. Add the chopped beet and apples to the pan along with the sugar, salt, raisins and the rest of the vinegar. Cook gently on low heat stirring all the while until a chutney consistency is reached.

3. Remove from fire, pour into hot sterilised jars and seal.

BITTER GOURD

1. **Karela Achar (North Indian)**

2. **Bitter Gourd Pickle (Anglo-Indian)**

3. **Bitter Gourd Pickle (Without Oil)**

4. **Bitter Gourd Garlic Chutney**

5. **Hagalkai Gojju (Karnataka)**

Karela Achar (North Indian)

Ingredients

300 gm bitter gourd
1/2 tsp turmeric powder
oil, preferably mustard
salt to taste

Powder roughly all together

1 tbsp onion seeds (kalonji)
1/2 tbsp fenugreek (methi)
1 tbsp aniseed (saunf)
8-10 red chillies
a small piece of turmeric (haldi)

Method

1. Scrape, wash and cut the bitter gourd pieces of desired size, sprinkle the turmeric powder and some salt, and leave aside for 1 1/2-2 hours.

2. Strain the gourd pieces to remove water, and discard this water. Wash the gourd pieces thoroughly. Dry on a clean cloth in the hot sun for a few hours until the pieces are dry.

3. Mix the powdered masalas with some salt. Put these in a clean jar along with the dried pieces of gourd and mix thoroughly.

4. Pour enough oil to cover the pieces. Shake the jar well so that the gourd and masalas blend together. Cover the mouth of the jar. If desired the oil can be heated, cooled thoroughly and then poured into the jar. This pickle can be used after 2-3 days.

Bitter Gourd Pickle (Anglo-Indian)

Ingredients	Grind to paste in 4 tablespoons vinegar
1/4 kg bitter gourd	3 tsp mustard seeds
1/2 tsp turmeric powder	1 1/2 tsp cumin seeds
5-6 tbsp oil	1/4 tsp pepper
1/2 cup vinegar	6-8 red chillies
1 big piece of jaggery	8 cloves garlic
2 sprigs curry leaves	1" piece ginger
salt to taste	

Method

1. Wash and slit the gourds, remove the seeds and cut into 1" pieces.

2. Heat 2 tablespoons of oil in a kadai, and add the curry leaves and gourd pieces along with the turmeric powder. Fry on low heat till lightly browned. Remove from kadai and set aside.

3. Pour the rest of the oil into the kadai, add the ground paste and stir until the oil surfaces. Add the gourd pieces and stir for another 1-2 minutes.

4. Now add the rest of the vinegar, jaggery and salt, and cook on low heat till thick and of chutney consistency. Cool and bottle.

Bitter Gourd Pickle (Without Oil)

Ingredients   **Grind in 4 tbsp vinegar**

1/4 kg bitter gourd   2 tsp mustard seeds
3/4 cup vinegar   4-6 red chillies
a small piece of jaggery   6 cloves garlic
salt to taste   half-inch piece ginger

Method

1. Wash, wipe dry and slit the gourds. Remove the seeds, and cut into 1" pieces. Put into pan. Add 1/4 cup vinegar and boil for 5-7 minutes or until tender.

2. Mix the ground paste with the rest of the vinegar. Add the salt and jaggery, and boil a further 3-8 minutes.

3. Add the gourd pieces along with the vinegar, and simmer gently until a chutney consistency is reached. Remove from fire, cool and bottle.

Note

If you do not like the bitter taste discard the vinegar in which the gourd was cooked, adding only the gourd with some vinegar in step 3.

Bitter Gourd Garlic Chutney

Ingredients

1/4 kg bitter gourd   3-4 tbsp oil
3 green chillies, slit   1 tsp ginger garlic paste
1 large onion, minced   1/2 tsp turmeric powder
15-20 cloves garlic, peeled   1 tsp chilly powder
2-3 sprigs curry leaves   a pinch of pepper powder
a big piece of jaggery   1 tsp mustard seeds
lemon-size ball of tamarind   salt to taste

Method

1. Cut the bitter gourd into two halves, remove the inside white pulp and seeds, and cut into small pieces.

2. Sprinkle some salt and 1/4 teaspoon of turmeric powder, mix with the gourd pieces, and set aside for 3-4 hours.

3. Heat 2 tablespoons of oil in a kadai, and fry the pieces to a brownish colour. (If you do not like the bitter taste, squeeze the pieces and discard the juice. Wash the gourd pieces in water two or three times and then fry.) Remove the fried pieces from the kadai and set aside.

4. Boil the tamarind in water, and take out the extract. Dry roast the mustard, powder, and set aside.

5. Heat the rest of the oil in a kadai, add the slit chillies, curry leaves, onion and garlic, and fry till the onions are browned.

6. Now add the ginger-garlic paste and the rest of the turmeric powder along with the chilly and pepper powders. Continue to fry until the oil surfaces.

7. Add the tamarind extract, jaggery, salt and fried gourd pieces, and simmer until a chutney consistency is reached. Add the mustard powder, mix, and remove from fire. Cool and bottle. Refrigerated, it will keep for a month.

Hagalkai Gojju (Karnataka)
(sweet sour bitter gourd chutney)

Ingredients   **Fry in 1 teaspoon of oil and powder smooth**

1/4 kg bitter gourd   1 tsp urad dal
1/2 tsp turmeric powder   1 tsp channa dal
1 lemon-sized ball of tamarind   1 tsp sesame seeds
2 sprigs curry leaves   1/4 tsp fenugreek seeds
2 green chillies, slit (optional)   1/2 cup grated copra
4 tbsp oil (til)   2-3 red chillies
1 small piece of jaggery   1/2 tsp cumin seeds
salt to taste

Method

1. Wash the bitter gourd, slit, remove the seeds and cut into small pieces.

2. Heat the oil and fry the gourd pieces until they are crisp and brown in colour. Set aside.

3. Boil the tamarind in water, and take out the extract. Boil this along with the turmeric powder, salt, jaggery and curry leaves. When sufficiently boiled it will have reduced to half the original quantity.

4. Add the gourd pieces and prepared powder, and simmer all together until thick and of a chutney consistency. Refrigerated, it will keep 1-2 weeks.

BRINJAL

1. **Brinjal Pickle (West Bengal)**

2. **Baigan Ka Salan (Parsi Style)**

3. **Brinjal Pickle (Anglo-Indian)**

Brinjal Pickle (West Bengal)

Ingredients	Dry roast and powder coarsely
8 medium brinjals	1 tbsp onion seeds
a lemon-sized ball of tamarind	1 tbsp cumin seeds
4-6 tbsp mustard oil	1 tbsp aniseeds
1 tsp turmeric powder	1 tbsp fenugreek seeds
1 small piece of jaggery	
6-8 red chillies (or to taste)	
1 cup vinegar	
salt to taste	

Method

1. Wash, wipe dry and slit the brinjals lengthwise into 4-8 pieces, each as desired.

2. Sprinkle some salt and 1/2 teaspoon of turmeric powder, and leave aside for an hour or so.

3. Grind the tamarind in vinegar to a paste.

4. When about to fry, take the brinjal pieces between your palms, and squeeze gently to remove all water. Dab with a paper towel or cloth to remove all the moisture.

5. Heat half of the oil, add the brinjal slices and fry to a light brown. Remove from kadai and set aside.

6. Pour the rest of the oil into the kadai, break each chilly into 2-3 pieces, add to the oil and fry until dark brown in colour.

7. Add the prepared powder, stir fry for 1-2 minutes, and when the oil surfaces, add the tamarind paste along with the jaggery and salt, and boil for 1-2 additional minutes.

8. Add the fried brinjal pieces and simmer gently until well blended and a chutney consistency has been reached.

9. Remove from fire, and allow to cool thoroughly. Pour into sterilised pickle jar and seal.

Baigan Ka Salan (Parsi Style)

Ingredients	**Grind together in 4 tbsp vinegar**
1/2 kg green long brinjal	2 tsp mustard seeds
8-10 green chillies	1 1/2 tsp cumin seeds
2 sprigs of curry leaves	4-6 red chillies (dry)
6 tbsp oil	2 onions chopped
1 tsp turmeric powder	10-12 cloves garlic
1 lemon-sized ball of tamarind	1" piece ginger chopped
2-3 tbsp of powdered jaggery	
salt to taste	

Method

1. Soak the red chillies, mustard and cumin seeds in vinegar and when the chillies have turned soft, grind to a paste adding the rest of the ingredients. Set aside the ground paste.

2. Slit the brinjals full length, then cut into 1-1 1/2" pieces or as desired. Slit the chillies half way. Sprinkle some salt, 1/2 teaspoon of turmeric powder on the brinjal slices, cover, and keep aside for 30 minutes.

3. Boil the tamarind in water, and take out the extract.

4. Remove the brinjal slices from the brine, press each one lightly to remove excess water, and keep aside.

5. Heat the oil, add the curry leaves and green chillies, and when done, add the ground paste, the rest of the turmeric powder and fry on low heat stirring all the while until the oil surfaces.

6. Add the brinjal slices and continue to fry until they turn soft.

7. Add the rest of the ingredients and simmer on low heat until a chutney consistency is reached.

8. Remove from fire, cool and bottle.

Note

If desired 2 medium tomatoes (chopped) can be added in step 6 after the brinjals are done. Refrigerated, it will keep a month or so.

Brinjal Pickle (Anglo-Indian)

Ingredients

500 gm brinjal (round, purple variety)	1 tbsp cumin seeds
30 gm ginger	1 tbsp mustard seeds
30 gm garlic	1 small piece turmeric
8-10 green chillies (slit)	or 2 tsp turmeric powder
3 sprigs curry leaves	10-12 dried red chillies
1 cup oil	or 1 1/2 -2 tbsp chilly powder
1 1/2 cups vinegar	1 tsp fenugreek seeds
	2 tbsp + 2 tsp salt
	1/4 cup sugar

Method

1. Wash, wipe dry the brinjals, and cut them into large pieces. Smear 2 teaspoons of salt and leave aside for 2 to 3 hours.

2. If you are using red chillies, soak them in some vinegar along with the turmeric sticks, cumin and mustard seeds till the chillies turn soft.

3. Grind them along with half of the ginger and garlic to a smooth paste. Set aside.

4. Dry roast the fenugreek seeds, powder, and set aside.

5. Mince fine the other half of the ginger and garlic.

6. Heat the oil, add the slit chillies and curry leaves, and when done, the minced garlic and ginger. Fry for one to two minutes. Add the ground paste and continue to fry till the oil surfaces.

7. Press the brinjal slices between the palms of your hand to remove excess water. Add them to the ground paste and stir fry on low heat for a while.

8. When the brinjals are done add salt, sugar and any left over vinegar, and simmer until the gravy is thick.

9. Remove from fire, cool thoroughly and bottle.

CABBAGE

1. **Pickled Cabbage (Western)**

2. **Pickled Cabbage (Chinese)**

Pickled Cabbage (Western)

Ingredients

1 large cabbage
spiced vinegar (refer to the recipe for pickled beetroot)
salt to taste

Method

1. Wash and shred the cabbage, put a layer of shreds into a glass bowl, and sprinkle a layer of salt. Repeat until all the cabbage has been salted. Cover the bowl and leave aside for 24 hours.

2. Prepare the spiced vinegar and keep it ready.

3. Next day, remove the cabbage shreds from the bowl, and drain the salt water thoroughly. When fully drained, put the cabbage shreds into a jar and pour spiced vinegar to cover completely. Cover jar with a lid and leave aside for a couple of days before serving.

Note

Use red cabbage if available. The pickle will be crisper.

Pickled Cabbage (Chinese)

Ingredients

2 cups minced cabbage
2 green chillies, minced
1/2 tsp sugar
3 tbsp vinegar
a pinch of pepper powder
salt to taste

Method

1. Wash and wipe clean an earthen jar or wide-mouthed earthen pot. Put all the ingredients into it and shake thoroughly. Cover tight and leave aside overnight.

2. Serve the next day with Chinese food. Refrigerated, it will keep for a few days.

CAPSICUM

1.   **Capsicum Chilly Gojju (Tamil Nadu)**

2.   **Capsicum Pickle (Anglo-Indian)**

3.   **Pickled Capsicums (Mexican)**

Capsicum Chilly Gojju (Tamil Nadu)
(a spicy chutney with capsicum and green chillies)

Ingredients

250 gm capsicum
25 gm green chillies
1 lemon-sized piece of jaggery
1 lemon-sized ball of tamarind
4 tablespoons oil
1 tsp turmeric
salt to taste

For the seasoning

1 tsp mustard seeds
1/2 tsp fenugreek seeds
1/4 tsp asafoetida powder
2 sprigs curry leaves

Method

1.   Cut each chilly into two or three pieces. Cut the capsicum into pieces of the desired size. Boil the tamarind in water, and squeeze to extract the pulp.

2.   Heat the oil. Add the mustard, fenugreek and asafoetida and when done, add the curry leaves and green chillies and fry for a minute or two.

3.   Now add the capsicum and turmeric powder and fry for another minute. Add the tamarind pulp, jaggery, salt and 1 1/2 cups of water, and cook on low heat until a thick consistency is formed.

Capsicum Pickle (Anglo-Indian)

Ingredients	Grind to a paste in vinegar
1/4 kg capsicum	15 gm ginger
120 gm oil (about 1 cup)	15 gm garlic
1 1/4-1 1/2 cups vinegar	1 tsp turmeric powder
3 tsp sugar	1-1 1/2 tbsp chilly powder
salt to taste	1 tbsp cumin seeds powder

Method

1. Wash, wipe and slit the capsicums, remove the seeds, and cut into medium-sized pieces.

2. Heat half the oil in a kadai, add the curry leaves and capsicums, and fry on low heat until lightly browned. Remove the capsicums and set aside.

3. Pour the rest of the oil into the kadai, add the ground paste, and fry till the oil surfaces.

4. Add the salt, sugar and the rest of the vinegar, and simmer until a chutney consistency is reached.

5. Remove the kadai from fire, cool and bottle.

Note

Refrigerated, it will keep a fortnight.

Pickled Capsicums (Mexican)

Ingredients

3 cups capsicums (cut into chunks)
1/2 cup sliced onions

Boil together

1 cup vinegar
1 cup sugar
1 tsp mustard seeds
1 tsp celery seeds
5 cloves garlic, minced
1/2 tsp salt
1 pinch of turmeric powder

Method

1. Place the capsicums and onions in a jar.

2. Pour hot, spiced vinegar into jar to cover the pieces fully.

3. Allow to cool, cover and refrigerate.

CARROT

1. **Carrot Pickle (South Indian)**

2. **Carrot Pickle (West Bengal)**

3. **Carrot Pickle (Anglo-Indian)**

4. **Carrot Chutney (Anglo-Indian)**

5. **Carrot Murabba (North Indian)**

Carrot Pickle (South Indian)

Ingredients

3 carrots, chopped
1 tsp chilly powder
1/2 tsp turmeric powder
juice of 1 lemon
salt to taste

Seasoning

3 tsp oil
1/2 tsp mustard seeds
1/2 tsp fenugreek seeds
a large piece of asafoetida

Method

1. Place the chopped carrots in a bowl. Put the turmeric and chilly powder in the centre of the pieces.

2. Heat the oil, fry the fenugreek seeds and asafoetida, remove, powder, and set aside.

3. To the same oil add the mustard and when done, pour the hot oil on the chilly-turmeric powders. Add salt, lemon juice and the prepared powders, mix thoroughly and bottle.

Note

Refrigerated, it will keep for a week.

Carrot Pickle (West Bengal)

Ingredients

500 gm carrots	2 bay leaves
about 1/2 cup oil	1 tbsp aniseeds
(preferably mustard oil)	a few black cardamom seeds
1 tbsp salt (or to taste)	1 tbsp chilly powder
1 tbsp minced ginger	1/2 tsp turmeric powder
a pinch of asafoetida	

Method

1. Wash, wipe and cut the carrots into 1" pieces.

2. Heat the oil, add the bay leaves, asafoetida and aniseeds and when done add the carrot pieces, ginger and turmeric powder, and fry for 3-5 minutes on low heat stirring all the while.

3. Now add the chilly powder, cardamom seeds and salt, and fry further for a few minutes. Cook until the carrots are tender, remove from fire, cool thoroughly and bottle. Refrigerated, it will keep 1-2 weeks.

Carrot Pickle (Anglo-Indian)

Ingredients

500 gm carrots	12-15 dried red chillies
3 tsp mustard seeds	1 cup oil
3 tsp cumin seeds	1/4 cup sugar
30 gm ginger	1 1/2-2 tbsp salt
30 gm garlic	1 cup vinegar

Method

1. Scrape, wash and cut the carrots into 1" pieces.

2. Soak all the masalas in 3/4 cup vinegar for 1 hour or so, then grind to a paste.

3. Heat the oil, add the ground paste and fry on low heat until the oil surfaces.

4. Add the salt, sugar and the remaining vinegar. Cook on low heat till the carrots become tender, and the gravy becomes thick.

5. Remove from heat, cool thoroughly and bottle.

Carrot Chutney (Anglo-Indian)

Ingredients

1/2 kg carrots, grated	3 cloves
2 tbsp black raisins (dried)	3 black cardamoms
1 tsp minced garlic	1" stick cinnamon
1 tsp minced ginger	a small piece of jaggery
1 1/2-2 tbsp chilly powder	1 1/2 cups vinegar
(or to taste)	1 1/2 tbsp salt (or to taste)
1/2 tsp turmeric powder	

Method

1. Spread the carrot gratings on a plate and keep this in the sun for a few hours or until the gratings are dry and there is no moisture left.

2. Tie the spices in a spice bag (or a thin muslin cloth) along with the ginger and garlic.

3. Pour the vinegar into a thick-bottomed saucepan. Add the turmeric, chilly powder, salt, jaggery and spice bag. Boil this for three to five minutes. Cool, remove spice bag, squeeze to get all the liquid, and discard bag.

4. Cool the spiced vinegar, pour over the carrots, mix thoroughly and bottle.

Carrot Murabba (North Indian)

Ingredients

1/4 kg carrots	1/2 tsp citric acid
1/4 kg sugar	rose or kewra essence

Method

1. Scrape the carrots, wash thoroughly, and wipe with a clean cloth. Cut into rounds or 1" length pieces. Prick the pieces with a sharp needle.

2. Put the pieces into a ceramic bowl, sprinkle sugar and leave overnight.

3. Next day, add the citric acid and bring to a boil on very, very low heat until the carrots turn soft and the syrup forms a one-thread consistency.

4. Remove from fire, add the essence, cool, pour into sterilised jars, and seal.

CUCUMBER

---

1.   **Pickled Cucumbers (Western)**

2.   **Pickled Cucumbers (Chinese)**

3.   **Spicy Pickled Cucumbers (Anglo-Indian)**

Pickled Cucumbers (Western)

Ingredients

1 medium cucumber
2 tbsp salt
1 1/4 cups spiced vinegar (refer to the recipe for pickled beetroot)

Method

1. Wash, peel and cut the cucumber into chunks. Sprinkle the salt, and put into a bowl. Leave overnight.

2. Next day, drain all the salt water, wash pieces thoroughly in cold water, drain and leave on a clean cloth to remove all moisture.

3. Put the pieces into a jar. Pour sufficient cooled, spiced vinegar to cover the pieces, cover the jar and seal.

Pickled Cucumbers (Chinese)

Ingredients

1 large cucumber
4 green chillies, minced
1/2" piece ginger, minced
3 cloves garlic, minced
a pinch of sugar
2 tbsp vinegar
2 tbsp water
salt and pepper to taste

Method

1. Wash, wipe and peel the cucumber. Cut into chunks or lengthwise pieces as desired. Place in a clean jar, add the minced chillies, and set aside for some time.

2. In a pan add the rest of the ingredients, and set to boil. Boil for 3-5 minutes, remove from fire, and cool.

3. Pour cooled, spiced vinegar over the chilly-cucumber pieces, and mix thoroughly.
   Cover the jar. It can be served after a couple of hours.

Spicy Pickled Cucumbers (Anglo-Indian)

Ingredients

1/2 kg tiny cucumbers
1 cup vinegar
1/2 tsp salt
2 tsp sugar

Tie spices in a bag

3-4 green chillies, minced
1" ginger, minced
1 tsp minced dill weed
2-3 cloves
1/2 " cinnamon stick
a few peppercorns

Method

1. Wash and peel the cucumbers. If small keep them whole, otherwise cut into 2" pieces or to required size. Put them into an earthenware jar or glass bottle, and set aside.

2. To the spice bag, add the vinegar along with salt and sugar, and simmer for a while. Remove from fire, and allow to cool.

3. Pour the cooled, spiced vinegar into the jar fully covering the pieces, and leave aside for two days.

4. On the third day drain the liquid, boil this once again, cool, pour over pieces, and cover. Use after a couple of hours.

DATE

```
1.   Date Chutney (Anglo-Indian)

2.   Date Carrot Chutney

3.   Pickled Dates (Western)
```

Date Chutney (Anglo-Indian)

Ingredients

250 gm dates	2" piece ginger, sliced
125 gm brown sugar	6 cloves garlic, minced
1/2-3/4 cup vinegar	1 tbsp chilly powder
1 tbsp almonds	a pinch of garam masala
1 tbsp raisins	2 tsp salt (or to taste)

Method

1. Cut the dates into halves and remove the stones. Cut into 2 or 3 pieces each. Blanch and sliver the almonds, clean the raisins, and set aside.

2. Mix the sugar in vinegar and gently heat for the sugar to dissolve.

3. When the sugar has dissolved completely, add the rest of the ingredients and simmer for 10-12 minutes or till a chutney consistency is reached.

4. Cool and bottle. Refrigerated, it will keep for about 2 weeks.

Date Carrot Chutney

Ingredients	Grind in vinegar
1/4 kg dates	1 large onion
1/4 kg carrots	1" piece ginger
1/2 kg brown sugar	3 cloves garlic, minced
125 gm raisins	1 tbsp chilly powder
2-2 1/2 cups vinegar	1 tbsp coriander powder
2-2 1/2 tsp salt (or to taste)	1/2" piece cinnamon
	3 cloves
	2 large cardamoms

Method

1. Stone the dates and cut into small pieces. Scrape, wash and cut the carrots to 1/2"-1" length pieces or to desired size. Clean the raisins.

2. Steam cook the carrots. When soft, remove from fire, and spread the pieces on a cloth to absorb moisture. Allow the pieces to get cool.

3. Mix together the ground paste, dates, carrots and the rest of the ingredients. Cook all together until the mixture reaches a chutney consistency.

4. Remove from fire, cool and bottle.

Pickled Dates (Western)

Ingredients

1/2 kg dates
1 1/4 cup spiced vinegar (refer to the recipe for pickled beetroot)
1 tsp salt (optional)

Method

1. Stone the dates, cut them into 4 lengthwise pieces, and put them into a jar or bottle.

2. To the hot spiced vinegar, add salt, mix, and pour this into jar. See that all the pieces are immersed in vinegar. Cover and seal.

DRUMSTICK

---

1.   **Drumstick Chutney (South Indian)**

2.   **Drumstick Pickle (Anglo-Indian)**

Drumstick Chutney (South Indian)

Ingredients

12-15 drumsticks
(good pulpy variety)
2 sprigs curry leaves
1/2-3/4 cup oil
a big lemon-sized ball
 of tamarind
a small piece of jaggery (optional)

1-1 1/2 tbsp chilly powder
1/2 tsp fenugreek seeds
a small bit of asafoetida
1/2 tsp mustard seeds
1/2 tsp turmeric powder
salt to taste

Method

1. Wash and cut the drumsticks into 3" pieces, add some water and cook until soft. Scoop out the pulp and set aside.

2. Boil the tamarind in a little water, take out thick pulp, and set aside.

3. Heat a teaspoon of oil, and fry the fenugreek seeds and asafoetida. Remove from kadai, cool, powder, and set aside.

4. Heat the rest of the oil, add the mustard and when done, add the curry leaves and drumstick pulp along with the turmeric. Fry on low heat until the oil surfaces.

5. Add the tamarind pulp, chilly powder, salt and jaggery, and simmer on low heat until a chutney consistency is reached. Add the prepared powder mix.

6. Remove from fire, cool and bottle. Refrigerated, it will keep a couple of months.

Drumstick Pickle (Anglo-Indian)

Ingredients	Grind to paste in 1/2 cup vinegar
1/2 kg very tender drumsticks	1" piece ginger
2 sprigs curry leaves	10-12 cloves garlic
3/4-1 cup oil	1 tbsp cumin seeds
1/2 tsp turmeric powder	1 tbsp mustard seeds
1 cup vinegar	1/2 tsp fenugreek seeds
1 tsp salt or to taste	10-12 dried chillies
1 tsp sugar	

Method

1. The drumsticks should be very tender with the seeds not yet formed. Wash and wipe dry the drumsticks. Cut each into 2" or 3" pieces, and set aside.

2. Heat the oil, add the curry leaves and drumstick pieces, and fry for 2-3 minutes until the drumsticks have become slightly soft.

3. Add the ground paste, and continue to stir fry on low heat until the oil surfaces.

4. Now add the rest of the vinegar, salt and sugar, and simmer on low heat for a while.

5. Remove from fire, cool and bottle.

GARLIC

1. **Garlic Pickle (Tamil Nadu)**

2. **Garlic Chutney (Andhra Pradesh)**

Garlic Pickle (Tamil Nadu)

Ingredients	Dry roast and powder
1/4 kg peeled garlic cloves	1 tsp mustard seeds
juice of 4 lemons	1/2 tsp fenugreek seeds
1 1/2 tbsp powdered jaggery	1 tsp cumin seeds
1 1/2-2 tbsp chilly powder	1 tbsp coriander seeds
1/2 tsp turmeric powder	a small piece of asafoetida
1 1/2-2 tbsp salt	
3/4-1 cup oil	

Method

1. Heat the oil, add the garlic cloves and saute on low heat along with the turmeric powder until they turn soft.

2. Add the lemon juice and simmer gently.

3. When the garlic is done, add the chilly powder, jaggery and salt, and allow to simmer.

4. Lastly add the powdered masala, and mix thoroughly. Remove from fire, cool and bottle.

Garlic Chutney (Andhra Pradesh)

Ingredients

125 gm peeled garlic cloves
1 small ball of tamarind
1 tsp powdered jaggery
2 tsp oil
salt to taste
1 tsp mustard seeds
2 tsp urad dal
1 small piece of asafoetida
1/2 tsp fenugreek seeds
8-10 red chillies

Method

1. Heat 1 teaspoon of oil, add the mustard and when done, add the urad dal, asafoetida, fenugreek and red chillies. Fry to a dark brown colour. Remove, cool and powder roughly.

2. Heat the rest of the oil, add the garlic cloves and fry on low heat, stirring all the while until they have turned soft. Remove and cool.

3. Lightly fry the tamarind and salt, remove from kadai, and cool.

4. Mix together the jaggery, tamarind, salt and garlic cloves, and run in a mixer until done. Add the powdered masalas, and run once again until all of it is well blended. Remove and bottle.

GINGER

1. **Ginger Green Chilly Pickle (Tamil Nadu)**

2. **Ginger Chutney (Andhra Pradesh)**

3. **Ginger Murabba (North Indian)**

4. **Ginger Lemon**

Ginger Green Chilly Pickle (Tamil Nadu)

Ingredients

> 1 large piece of ginger
> 5-6 green chillies
> 2 large lemons
> salt to taste (about 2 1/2 tsp)
> 2 tsp oil
> a pinch of mustard

Method

1. Scrape and wash the ginger thoroughly, and cut into thin slivers (about 1 cup). Put these into a bowl.

2. Wash, wipe and cut the chillies into 2-3 pieces each.

3. Heat the oil, add the mustard and when done, add the green chillies and saute for one to two minutes or till they turn soft. Transfer this to the bowl.

4. Extract the juice of the lemons, add salt and mix this along with the ginger and chillies, and transfer to a bottle. Refrigerated, it will keep for one to two weeks.

Ginger Chutney (Andhra Pradesh)

Ingredients

100 gm ginger (about 3 large pieces)
12 cloves peeled garlic
2 tbsp coriander powder
2 tsp cumin seed powder
1 large ball of tamarind
4 tsp oil
2 sprigs curry leaves
1 tsp salt

Method

1. Wash, scrape and chop the ginger. Mince the garlic. In 1 teaspoon of oil, fry the ginger and garlic until they turn soft. Remove from kadai, and cool.

2. Add the tamarind and salt to the fried ginger and garlic, and grind to a paste.

3. Heat the rest of the oil, and add the curry leaves and ground paste. Stir fry adding the coriander and cumin powders. Continue to fry until the oil surfaces. Cool and bottle.

Ginger Murabba (North Indian)

Ingredients

150 gm ginger
250 gm sugar
juice of 2 large lemons
1 tbsp honey
a few drops lemon essence
2-3 drops yellow food colour

Method

1. Scrape, wash and cut the ginger into slivers. Add enough water to cover the pieces, and cook until soft. Strain the water, and set aside the pieces. Strain the lemon juice, and set aside.

2. Add sugar to the ginger water, and allow to dissolve. Add some more water if necessary. Cook over low heat until the syrup is thick.

3. Add the lemon juice and ginger pieces, and cook further for 5-7 minutes. Do not allow the syrup to get too thick as it will crystallise.

4. Remove from fire, and add the honey, essence and colour. Mix thoroughly, cool and bottle.

5. Serve with chapatis or bread. It acts as a good digestive.

Ginger Lemon

Ingredients

> 1/2 cup ginger juice (2 tsp chopped ginger)
> 1 cup lemon juice (4-6 lemons)
> 2 cups sugar
> a few drops yellow food colour (optional)

Method

1. To two teaspoons of chopped ginger, add 1 cup of water, and grind to a smooth paste. Leave this in a cup for a while for the juice to settle down. Take the top portion only, discarding the sediment.

2. Add the sugar to the ginger juice, using some more water if necessary. Boil to a one-thread consistency, remove from fire, and cool thoroughly.

3. Add the lemon juice and food colour. Mix and bottle.

Note It makes a very refreshing drink on a hot day.

A delicious array of delicacies: jam, juice, chutney, marmalade and pickles

The 'raw material' (apples, oranges and apricots) and the 'finished products' (apple chutney, orange marmalade and apricot juice)

Delectable concentrates from apples and bananas

GREEN CHILLY

1. **Stuffed Green Chillies (North Indian)**

2. **Stuffed Green Chillies (Anglo-Indian)**

3. **Stuffed Red Chillies (North Indian)**

4. **Green Chilly Pickle (South Indian)**

5. **Milagai Thokku (Tamil Nadu)**

6. **Puli Milagai (Tamil Nadu)**

7. **Pickled Chillies (Chinese)**

Stuffed Green Chillies (North Indian)

Ingredients	Mix together
1/2 kg green chillies (long variety)	1 tbsp mustard powder
1/4 kg sesame seed oil (til oil)	1 tbsp fenugreek powder
100 gm salt	1 tbsp aniseed powder
	1/2 tbsp turmeric powder
	4 tbsp amchoor or lime juice
	2 tbsp salt

Method

1. Wash, wipe dry and slit the chillies right through to within half an inch of the end. Open the chilly carefully and stuff the above masala powders.

2. In a dry clean jar sprinkle a thin layer of salt to cover the entire bottom surface. On this spread the stuffed chillies. Repeat the process until both the salt and chillies are used up.

3. Heat the oil, remove from fire, and cool it thoroughly. Pour over the entire surface of chillies. Shake jar, cover with a clean cloth and leave in the sun for at least a week, then store.

Stuffed Green Chillies (Anglo-Indian)

Ingredients	Grind to paste in 2 tablespoons vinegar
1/4 kg long, green chillies	1 1/2" piece ginger
a lemon-sized ball of tamarind	12 cloves garlic
1 cup vinegar	**Broil, cool and powder roughly**
1 cup mustard oil	
1 tsp turmeric powder	1 tsp coriander seeds
1 tsp chilly powder	1/2 tsp fenugreek seeds
1 tsp pepper powder (optional)	a small piece of asafoetida
60 gm salt (or to taste)	1 tbsp mustard seeds

Method

1. Wash, wipe dry and slit each chilly up to the end of the stalk, keeping the stalk as it is.

2. After grinding the ginger-garlic paste in vinegar, boil the rest of the vinegar with tamarind. Cool, strain, and set aside.

3. Heat 3-4 tablespoons of oil, add the ground paste, and fry for a while adding the turmeric and chilly powders. Continue to fry adding the powdered masalas until the oil surfaces. Remove from fire, and cool.

4. Carefully stuff the chillies with this prepared masala paste. Place them in a jar in a layer. Pour over this the tamarind vinegar solution. Repeat the chilly and vinegar layers until both are used up. Shake jar gently for the chillies to settle down.

5. Heat the remaining oil, cool thoroughly, pour into jar, cover and store.

Stuffed Red Chillies (North Indian)

Ingredients

1/2 kg red chillies (long variety)
1 cup mustard oil

Broil each separate, then mix, cool, powder roughly

2 tbsp coriander seeds (dhania)
1 tbsp fenugreek seeds (methi)
1 tbsp onion seeds (kalaunji)
3 tbsp mustard seeds (rai)
1 tbsp aniseeds (saunf)
1 tbsp cumin seeds (jeera)

To the above masala power add

4 - 6 tbsp salt (or to taste)
1 tsp turmeric powder
1 tsp chilly powder (optional)

Method

1. Wash the chillies and wipe dry thoroughly using a paper towel or cloth. Wipe each separate. There should be no trace of water when you start making the pickle.

2. Slit each chilly carefully, removing the centre pip and all the seeds. Keep the seeds separate. **Sun** the chillies for a couple of hours or until they turn a little soft.

3. To the powdered masalas add 1/2 cup oil and the seeds kept by (either all of it or part of it as desired). Mix all together to form a rough dough.

4. Open each chilly carefully, stuff some of the above masala into each, and keep the stuffed chilly on a plate. Stuff all the chillies thus and if any stuffing is left over, keep aside.

5. **Sun** the chillies once again (in very hot sun) for a couple of hours until they turn slightly soft. Remove from the sun and cool.

6. Take a clean jar or a wide-mouthed bottle, dip each chilly in oil to coat fully and put this oiled chilly in the jar. Finish off all chillies thus. Any left over oil and masalas can be sprinkled all over the chillies. Cover the mouth of the jar and store.

Note

Carefully made, it will keep for a year.

Green Chilly Pickle (South Indian)

Ingredients

1/2 kg green chillies
a large ball of tamarind
1/4 kg oil (preferably til)
2 tsp turmeric powder
3-4 tbsp salt (to taste)

Broil and powder

1 1/2 tbsp mustard seeds
1 tbsp fenugreek seeds
1 tsp asafoetida piece
2 tbsp sesame seeds

Method

1. Boil the tamarind in a little water, and take out thick extract, removing the seeds and pips. Pass through a strainer, and set aside.

2. Wash and wipe dry the chillies thoroughly. There should be absolutely no traces of water. Slit each chilly into two, halfway through.

3. Heat the oil and when done, add the chillies and fry until soft. Do not allow to get browned.

4. Add the tamarind extract, and cook for a while.

5. Add the salt and powdered spices, and cook further until the oil surfaces. Cool and bottle.

Note

If the surface appears dry add some more oil, boiled and cooled.

Milagai Thokku (Tamil Nadu)
(green chilly chutney)

Ingredients

100 gm fresh, green chilllies
1 small ball of jaggery (powdered)
1 large lemon-sized ball of tamarind
1/2 cup oil
1 tbsp urad dal
1 small piece of asafoetida
1 tsp mustard
1 tbsp salt (or to taste)

Method

1. Snip each of the chillies, then wash and cut into 2 or 3 pieces each.

2. In 1 teaspoon of oil, fry the asafoetida and urad dal to brown. Remove, cool, powder, and set aside.

3. Add 1 tablespoon of oil to the kadai, and fry the cut chillies lightly to remove moisture. Do not allow to get browned.

4. Clean the tamarind removing the strands and fibre. Add the salt and fried chillies, and run in a mixer until lightly ground.

5. Add the prepared dal powder and jaggery, and run the mixer further until it is all blended. Remove.

6. Heat the rest of the oil, season with mustard, add the ground mixture and fry until dry. Remove from kadai, cool and bottle.

Note

This chutney keeps a long while.

Puli Milagai (Tamil Nadu)
(green chillies in tamarind sauce)

Ingredients

100 gm green chillies
1 large lemon-sized ball of tamarind
3-4 tsp salt or to taste
a small piece of jaggery
1/2 cup oil
1 tsp fenugreek seeds
a small piece of asafoetida
1 tsp mustard seeds
1/2 tsp turmeric powder
2 sprigs curry leaves

Method

1. Wash, wipe dry and slit each chilly half-way through.

2. Boil the tamarind in a little water, extract the pulp, strain, and set aside.

3. Heat 1 teaspoon of oil, and fry the asafoetida and fenugreek seeds to brown. Remove, cool, powder, and set aside.

4. Pour the rest of the oil into the kadai, add the mustard and when done, the curry leaves. Add the chillies and fry until they turn soft, on very low heat, stirring all the while, adding the turmeric powder while frying.

5. Add the tamarind pulp, simmer for some time, add the jaggery, and salt, and cook until the chutney is quite thick.

6. Add the prepared powder, mix, and remove from kadai.

7. Cool and bottle.

Note

You can add a few capsicums if desired in step 4.

Pickled Chillies (Chinese)

Ingredients

> 6-8 green chillies, minced fine
> 1/2 cup vinegar
> 1 tsp sugar
> a large pinch of salt

Method

1. In a bottle or earthen pot mix all the ingredients, shake the vessel and leave aside. Allow the chillies to marinate. Serve after a couple of hours with Chinese fried rice or noodles.

Note

If you require the pickle very hot then add only a pinch of sugar.

GOOSEBERRY

1.   **Salted Gooseberries (South Indian)**

2.   **Gooseberries in Oil (South Indian)**

3.   **Thair Nellikai (Tamil Nadu)**

4.   **Nellikai Thokku (Tamil Nadu)**

5.   **Nellikai Uragai (Andhra Pradesh)**

6.   **Amla Achar (North Indian)**

7.   **Amla Murabba (North Indian)**

Salted Gooseberries (South Indian)

Ingredients

1 kg gooseberries
150-200 gm salt
1 tsp turmeric powder

Method

1. Wash the gooseberries and set aside.

2. Boil enough water (to cover the berries), and add salt and turmeric powder. When it starts to boil, add the gooseberries and boil until they turn soft. Remove one from the water and press lightly. If the seed comes out easily, it is done.

3. Transfer the gooseberries into a wide-mouthed jar, cool thoroughly, then cover with a lid. Tie a clean muslin cloth around the lid, and leave aside.

4. When required, serve in any of the following ways, as described in some of the recipes that follow.

Note

The gooseberries can also be served as they are with curd rice. It is better to refrigerate as is, or season in any one of the following ways and refrigerate, as they do not last long without refrigeration.

Gooseberries in Oil (South Indian)

Ingredients

1 cup gooseberries (from the above recipe)
1/2-1 tsp chilly powder or to taste
1/4 tsp turmeric powder
1/4 cup oil
1 tsp mustard seeds

Fry in 1 tsp oil and powder

> 1/2 tsp fenugreek seeds
> a small piece of asafoetida

Method

1. Press each gooseberry carefully, remove the seed and discard. Keep the berries whole or break them into slices.

2. Heat the oil, add the mustard and when done, the gooseberries (whole or in slices), and fry carefully on low heat turning all the while. Add the turmeric and chilly powders while frying.

3. When sufficiently fried, add the prepared asafoetida and fenugreek powder, and mix thoroughly. When cool, add 1/2-1 cup water (as desired) from the jar in which the gooseberries have been kept. Mix, bottle and refrigerate.

Thair Nellikai (Tamil Nadu)
(gooseberries in curds)

Ingredients

> 1 cup gooseberries (from the first recipe)
> 1 1/2-2 cups curds (churned)
> 4-6 green chillies (slit)
> 2 tsp til oil (sesame seed oil)
> 1/2 tsp mustard seeds
> 1 sprig curry leaf
> a pinch of asafoetida powder
> a little salt

Method

1. Remove the gooseberries from the jar, deseed and keep aside.

2. Heat the oil, and add the mustard and asafoetida powder. When done, add the curry leaves and chillies, saute for 1-2 minutes, add the gooseberies and fry on low heat for 2-3 minutes turning all the while until sufficiently fried.

3. Remove from fire. Cool and add to the beaten curds with some salt if required. Can be served immediately.

Note Refrigerated it will keep 2-3 weeks.

Nellikai Thokku (Tamil Nadu)

Ingredients

1 cup chopped gooseberries
a few curry leaves
1/2 tsp turmeric powder
2 tsp chilly powder
1/2 tsp fenugreek seeds
1 small piece of asafoetida
1 tsp mustard seeds
1/2-3/4 cup oil
a little salt

Method

1. Remove the gooseberries from the jar (see the first recipe in this section), and chop and take one cup of it.

2. In 1 teaspoon of oil, fry the fenugreek and asafoetida, powder, and set aside.

3. Heat the oil, add the mustard and when done, the curry leaves and the chopped gooseberries. Fry on low heat adding the turmeric powder.

4. When the pieces have turned soft, add the chilly powder, salt (if required), the prepared powder, and fry for another 1-2 minutes until the whole is blended.

5. Remove from fire, cool and bottle.

Nellikai Uragai (Andhra Pradesh)
(gooseberry pickle)

Ingredients

> 1/4 kg gooseberries
> 10-12 green chillies
> 1 tbsp salt
> 1/2 tsp turmeric powder
> a piece of asafoetida
> 2 tbsp sesame seed oil (til)
> 1/2 tsp mustard seeds

Method

1. Remove the salted gooseberries from the jar (as prepared in the first recipe of this section). Press each berry lightly to remove the seed, break into slices, and set aside.

2. Mix all the other ingredients except the oil and mustard, grind roughly, and set aside.

3. Heat the oil, add the mustard, and when done, add the ground masala, and stir 1-2 minutes. Add the gooseberry slices, fry for another 1-2 minutes, remove from fire, cool and bottle.

Amla Achar (North Indian)
(gooseberry pickle)

Ingredients

1 kg gooseberries	**Broil and powder roughly**

Ingredients   **Broil and powder roughly**

1 kg gooseberries   1 tbsp onion seeds
1/2 kg mustard oil   1 tbsp aniseeds
1/2 cup chilly powder   2 tbsp cumin seeds
2 tsp turmeric powder   3 tbsp mustard seeds
1/2 cup salt (or to taste)   a small piece of asafoetida

Method

1. Boil some water, add the gooseberries, simmer for 3-5 minutes. Remove from fire. Cover and leave aside for 5 minutes.

2. Drain out all the water. Rub salt and turmeric powder on the berries, put into a jar and leave aside for a day.

3. Next day, strain the water and leave the gooseberries in the sun for a whole day or two until berries are dried.

4. Put all the masalas on a plate. Add enough oil to hold together. Take a handful of berries at a time. Coat with the masala paste and put into a jar. Finish all the berries and masalas thus. If any masala is left over, sprinkle on top.

5. Pour the left over oil on top, leave jar in the sun for a whole week until the berries and masalas are blended. Cover and store.

Amla Murabba (North Indian)

Ingredients

1/2 kg gooseberries
1 kg sugar
a large pinch of cardamom powder
1/2 tsp lime (also known as chunnam or Calcium Carbonate)

Method

1. Wash the gooseberries and drain the water. Prick each one with a sharp needle and set aside.

2. Dissolve lime in plenty of water, immerse berries in it and set aside for 2-3 hours.

3. Drain all the lime (chunnam) water, wash the berries two to three times in fresh water, strain once again, and set aside.

4. To 1 1/2 cups of water add sugar to make a thick syrup of one thread consistency. While making the syrup remove the scum forming on top from time to time.

5. Put in the gooseberries and cook over low heat stirring all the while until syrup is very thick. Add the cardamom powder, mix, and leave aside to cool.

6. When cooled thoroughly, transfer to a wide-mouthed bottle, cover and store. Note that an amla a day, prepared this way, taken in the morning, gives the necessary Vitamin C for the day.

GUAVA

---

1. **Guava Jelly**

2. **Guava Cheese**

Guava Jelly

Ingredients

1 kg guava
sugar
10 gm citric acid
a little red food colour (optional)

Method

1. Wash the guavas and cut into small pieces using a stainless steel knife as otherwise the pieces will turn black.

2. Add sufficient water to cover the fruit. Add half of the citric acid and boil for 20-30 minutes till the fruit has become very soft. Remove from fire, and cool.

3. Collect the cooked pulp in a muslin cloth or a thin towel, tie the open ends securely (like a bag) and hang this on a peg allowing the extract to fall in droplets into a bowl at bottom. Since this process takes a very long time, it is better to leave this overnight. Never press the bag to hurry the extraction or this will cloud the end product.

4. When the extract has come through fully, add to this the rest of the citric acid and sugar. For every cup of extract use 3/4 cup sugar. Cook this stirring until the sugar has dissolved.

5. Once the sugar has dissolved, boil for a minute, remove from fire, and strain the syrup through a muslin cloth. Add the colour, mix and put back on fire.

6. Now cook the mixture further without stirring until you get a sheet consistency. Test for this. Refer to the instructions for setting jelly to be found in the introduction to this book.

7. Remove from fire and pour into hot, sterilised bottles. Leave the bottles open until jelly cools, then seal and cover.

Guava Cheese

Ingredients

1 cup cooked guava pulp (after straining)
3/4-1 cup sugar (according to taste)
1 tbsp butter
1/4 tsp citric acid or juice of a lemon
a few drops red food colour (optional)

Method

1. Wash and cut the guavas into small pieces using a stainless steel knife. Add enough water to cover the fruit and cook until soft. Cool, smash and strain pulp, discarding the seeds and skin. Measure the pulp and take the rest of the ingredients as above.

2. To the pulp add the sugar, butter, citric acid or lemon juice, and cook until a 'soft ball' stage is reached. A little bit put on a ceramic plate should form a soft ball when cool.

3. Remove from fire, add the colour, and mix thoroughly. Pour the mixture onto a greased plate, and cut into squares. Wrap each piece in butter paper and store.

Note

If you wish to make toffee, cook further to a hard ball shape. Remove from fire, take piece and roll with your finger to make toffee.

HERBS

1. **Coriander Dry Chutney (Tamil Nadu)**

2. **Coriander Garlic Dry Chutney (Andhra Pradesh)**

3. **Curry Leaf Tamarind Chutney (Tamil Nadu)**

4. **Curry Leaf Garlic Chutney Powder (Andhra Pradesh)**

5. **Dill Cucumber Pickle (Western)**

6. **Mint Apple Chutney (Western)**

7. **Mint Syrup**

8. **Minty Sauce**

Coriander Dry Chutney (Tamil Nadu)

Ingredients

1 large bundle fresh coriander leaves
1 lemon-sized ball tamarind (break into small pieces)
1-1 1/2 tsp salt
1 tbsp til oil

Fry in 1 teaspoon oil to golden brown

1 1/2 tbsp urad dal
a small piece of asafoetida
4- 5 whole red chillies (to taste)

Method

1. Pick the coriander leaves, discard the thick stalks, and wash thoroughly to remove all grit. Drain the water and spread on a cloth to remove all moisture.

2. After frying the chillies and dal, remove, and pour the rest of the oil into the kadai. Gently stir the leaves on very low heat until they are absolutely dry. Remove from fire, and allow to cool.

3. In a mixer run the fried chillies, asafoetida and tamarind. Then add salt, coriander leaves and the fried dal, and run again for 1-2 minutes until all the ingredients are well blended.

4. Remove and bottle. It will keep 1-2 weeks, refrigerated.

Coriander Garlic Dry Chutney (Andhra Pradesh)

Ingredients

1/2 kg coriander leaves
120 gm tamarind
1/2 cup salt
3-4 tsp chilly powder
a few cloves garlic, peeled
1/2-3/4 cup oil

Method

1. Pick and wash the coriander leaves thoroughly, drain the water and leave on a cloth or paper towel to remove all moisture. When thoroughly dried, discard the thick stems, and chop.

2. Heat the oil, add the chopped leaves and saute on very low heat stirring all the while until completely dry. Remove from fire, and allow to cool.

3. Clean the tamarind, break into small pieces and stir fry along with salt in a dry kadai until all the moisture has dried up.

4. Remove the tamarind from the kadai, and allow to cool. Add the peeled garlic cloves, the rest of the ingredients, and run all of it in a mixer until well blended. Remove and bottle.

Note

Will keep for a long while if properly prepared with no traces of moisture.

Curry Leaf Tamarind Chutney (Tamil Nadu)

Ingredients   **Seasoning**

2 cups picked curry leaves   4 tbsp oil
1 small ball of tamarind   1/2 tsp mustard seeds
salt to taste   1 tsp urad dal

Fry in 1 teaspoon oil

1 tsp peppercorns
1/2 tsp cumin seeds
6 red chillies

Method

1. Wash the leaves thoroughly, and leave in a colander for the water to drain.

2. Take out the extract of tamarind - approximately 1-1 1/2 cups.

3. Grind to a paste the fried ingredients along with the curry leaves and salt.

4. Heat the oil, add the mustard seeds and dal. When done, add the ground paste, tamarind extract and some more water if too thick.

5. Allow the chutney to boil on slow heat for 20-30 minutes or until a thick chutney consistency is reached. Remove, cool and bottle.

Note   Refrigerated it will keep 2 weeks.

Curry Leaf Garlic Chutney Powder (Andhra Pradesh)

Ingredients

2 cups picked curry leaves   1/2 tsp coriander seeds
4-6 garlic cloves   1/2 tsp cumin seeds
1 small ball of tamarind   1 tbsp urad dal
salt to taste   5-6 red chillies
1/2 tbsp ghee

Method

1. Wash the leaves, and spread on a cloth to dry - there should be no water while frying.

2. Heat the ghee, fry the masalas (ingredients on the right hand side) one at a time, removing each from the kadai as it is done.

3. When the masalas are fried, fry the curry leaves on slow heat - they should be fried but not browned. Allow to cool.

4. Grind together the tamarind, salt and garlic. When done, add the fried ingredients and curry leaves, and grind further until all the masalas are powdered and well blended. Remove and bottle.

Note

This powder is good for digestion - when taken with curd rice, it removes uneasiness of the stomach.

Dill Cucumber Pickle (Western)

Ingredients

    1 large bundle of dill
    200 gm very small cucumbers
    6 cloves garlic, sliced thinly
    1 cup vinegar, white preferably
    1 1/2 cups cold water
    1 tbsp salt
    a few peppercorns
    1-2 green chillies
    1 tsp sugar

Method

1. Wash the cucumbers thoroughly. Wipe dry with a clean cloth. Trim the ends, cut each into 3" pieces. Put them in a ceramic bowl, add water, cover, and leave overnight.

2. Next day, drain all the water, prick each piece with a sharp needle and spread on a clean cloth to dry thoroughly.

3. Pick and wash the dill discarding their stems, then chop the leaves fine.

4. In a clean dry jar, spread half the chopped dill and garlic slices, and cover the surface with the cucumber pieces. Spread the rest of the dill and garlic over the cucumber pieces.

5. Boil together the water, vinegar, salt and pepper for 2-3 minutes. Cool and pour this over the cucumber and dill layers, and seal the jar.

Mint Apple Chutney (Western)

Ingredients

1/2 kg cooking apples (sour variety)
150 gm sugar
1 tbsp finely chopped mint
1/2 tsp salt
1 cup white or malt vinegar

For the Spiced Vinegar

1 cup white or malt vinegar
5 cloves
1/2" stick cinnamon
a pinch of nutmeg

Tie together in a spice bag

1/2 tsp each of the following:
crushed black pepper
coriander seeds
1 small red chilly broken in two

Method

To Make the Spiced Vinegar

1. To one cup of vinegar add the spices and boil for some time until the flavour of the spices has been imparted to the vinegar. Remove from fire, leave aside for a few days, then strain and use.

2. Wash, wipe and chop the apples. Place them in a thick-bottomed saucepan. Add the vinegar and cook on low heat to boiling point.

3. Add the salt, sugar, and spice bag to the pan, then cook further until a chutney consistency is reached. Add the chopped mint, and mix thoroughly. Remove from fire. Pour into a hot sterilised jar and seal.

Mint Syrup

Ingredients

2 tbsp chopped mint
1/4 kg sugar
2 cups water
a little green food colour

Method

1. In a thick-bottomed pan put in the sugar and mint and mix well, crushing the mint to get the flavour.

2. Add water and stir vigorously to dissolve the sugar.

3. Set pan to boil and simmer for 12-15 minutes.

4. Now boil briskly for 3-5 minutes. Remove from fire. Cool and strain, then squeeze the mint leaves to extract maximum flavour.

5. Boil once again for 1-2 minutes. Add the colour, mix, and pour the hot syrup into sterilised bottles.

Note   If desired a few drops of lemon essence can be added for flavour in step 5.

Minty Sauce

Ingredients

1 cup picked mint leaves   1/2 tsp chilly powder
6 cloves garlic   1 1/2 tsp cumin powder
3 green chillies   1/4 tsp pepper powder
1" piece ginger   1 small lemon-sized ball of tamarind
salt to taste   a small piece of jaggery

Method

1. Grind to a paste all the ingredients on the left.

2. Extract thick pulp of tamarind by boiling in 1 cup of hot water.

3. To the tamarind extract add the ground paste, the powdered masalas and the jaggery. Simmer for 5-8 minutes or until a chutney consistency is reached.

4. Cool and bottle. It will keep for 1-2 weeks.

JACKFRUIT

---

1.   Jackfruit Mango Pickle (Bihar)

2.   Jackfruit Jam (Kerala)

Jackfruit Mango Pickle (Bihar)

Ingredients

1/2 kg jackfruit pieces	4 tbsp aniseeds
1/2 kg mango pieces	1/2 tbsp onion seeds
3/4-1 kg oil, preferably mustard	1 tsp fenugreek seeds
2 tsp turmeric powder	1 tbsp mustard seeds
3 tbsp chilly powder	1 piece of asafoetida
120-150 gm salt	

Method

1. With a sharp knife, remove the thick outer skin of the jackfruit, and cut into fairly large pieces. These should weigh 1/2 kg.

2. Wash, wipe and deseed the mangoes, and cut into large pieces. These should weigh 1/2 kg.

3. Keeping aside 1 tablespoon aniseeds whole, dry roast the rest of the masalas one by one until done. Cool thoroughly, and then powder roughly.

4. Heat some of the oil and stir fry the jackfruit pieces to a golden colour. Remove and cool thoroughly.

5. In the same oil put in the whole aniseeds and fry adding the turmeric and chilly powders. Stir for 1-2 minutes. Transfer this masala to the jackfruit pieces, add the mango pieces, salt and the roasted powdered masalas, and put all these into a jar.

6. Heat the rest of the oil, cool and pour over the ingredients in the jar. Mix thoroughly, cover the jar, **sun** and store.

Note

See that the pieces are immersed in oil. If not enough, heat and cool some more oil, and add to jar.

Jackfruit Jam (Kerala)
(palapaza pradaman)

Ingredients

1/2 kg fully ripe jackfruit segments
2 cups water
1 1/2- 2 cups jaggery

1/2 cup ghee or a little more
1 tsp powdered cardamom

Method

1. Chop the jackfruit segments into small pieces. Add water and cook until very soft, then mash thoroughly.

2. Powder the jaggery and add to the cooked fruit, stirring all the while. Simmer for a while until thick and the mixture starts to form a mass.

3. Gradually add the ghee, a little at a time, stirring all the while. When all the ghee has been added cook on low heat until the mixture starts to leave the sides of the vessel (as in the case of halwa).

4. Add the cardamom powder, mix, remove from fire and cool.

5. Grease a container thoroughly with ghee, transfer the jam into it, even out the surface, and pour some hot ghee on top. Cool thoroughly before covering. It will keep for a couple of months.

LEMON

1. **Salted Lemons**

2. **Seasoned Lemon Pickle (South Indian)**

3. **Instant Lime Pickle (South Indian)**

4. **Lime Green Chilly Ginger Pickle (South Indian)**

5. **Lemon Pickle (South Indian)**

6. **Lemon Thokku (Tamil Nadu)**

7. **Lemon Pickle with Green Spices (North Indian)**

8. **Lemon Pickle (North Indian)**

9. **Sweet and Sour Lemon Pickle (Anglo-Indian)**

10. **Seasoned Lime Pickle (Anglo-Indian)**

11. **Lemon Pickle (Sindhi Style)**

12. **Lemon Barley**

Salted Lemons

Ingredients

    25 large lemons
    1 1/2- 2 cups salt
    1 tsp turmeric powder

Method

1. Wash, wipe and cut 20 lemons into fours or eights as required. Take out juice of 5 lemons and set aside. Mix the salt and turmeric powder together.

2. In a clean jar put a layer of lemon pieces at the bottom, and sprinkle the salt-turmeric powder mixture. Put a second layer of lemon pieces, then again the salt, turmeric powder mixture. Repeat until all the pieces have been used up. Sprinkle any left over salt. Sprinkle the juice kept aside.

3. Cover the jar, tie a piece of muslin cloth and set aside. Keep in the sun for a day or two.

4. In this way the lemon can be preserved for a long while. You can either use it as is or you could take out the required quantity and season as described in the recipe below, when the pieces have become soft.

Seasoned Lemon Pickle (South Indian)

Ingredients

    1 cup lemon pieces (from the above recipe)
    1/2 tsp fenugreek seeds
    1 small piece of asafoetida
    8-10 red chillies (or to taste)
    1/2 tsp mustard seeds (powdered)
    1/2 tsp turmeric powder
    1/2 cup oil

Method

1. Heat a kadai, dry roast the fenugreek seeds to dark brown, and remove. Add one teaspoon of oil to the kadai, fry the asafoetida, remove. Add the chillies, saute one to two 2 minutes, and remove. Cool and powder all the three together. Set aside.

2. Heat the rest of the oil, add the mustard seeds and when done, add the lemon pieces along with the turmeric powder. Saute for 3-5 minutes.

3. Add the prepared powder, and gently mix all of these thoroughly. Add a little salt if necessary.

4. Remove from fire, cool and bottle.

Instant Lime Pickle (South Indian)

Ingredients

6 large limes
4 tsp salt
1 tbsp chilly powder
1/2 tsp turmeric powder
1 tbsp sesame seed oil
1/2 tsp mustard seeds

Fry in 1 tsp oil and powder fine

1/2 tsp fenugreek seeds
1 small piece of asafoetida

Method

1. Boil sufficient water to cover the limes when immersed. Add the turmeric powder and the limes, boil for 1-2 minutes, and remove vessel from fire. Cover and set aside.

2. When cooled, remove the limes, and cut each into 4 or 8 pieces as desired. Put these pieces into a bowl and cover the centre of the pieces with chilly powder.

3. Heat the oil, add the mustard and when done, pour the hot oil over the chilly powder so that it gets done.

4. Add the prepared fenugreek-asafoetida powder and salt, and mix thoroughly. If desired, add 1/2-1 cup water (in which the limes were boiled). Mix and bottle.

Note This pickle can be served immediately. Refrigerated, it will keep about a week.

Lime Green Chilly Ginger Pickle (South Indian)

Ingredients   **Fry in 1 tsp oil and powder fine**

15-20 large limes   1 tsp fenugreek seeds
100 gm green chillies (slit)   1/2 tsp mustard seeds
30 gm ginger (slivered)
1 tbsp sesame seed oil
1/2 tsp mustard seeds
1/2 cup salt (or to taste)

Method

1. Follow the recipe for Instant Lime Pickle and prepare the limes. Season as follows.

2. Heat the oil, add the mustard seeds and when done add the slit chillies, and saute for 1-2 minutes or until they turn soft but not dark. Add the ginger, fry for 1-2 more minutes, remove from fire, and cool.

3. Remove the limes from the vessel. Cut each into 4-8 pieces (as desired). Add salt if necessary, the seasoned ingredients, the prepared powder, mix thoroughly and bottle. It can be used immediately. Refrigerate.

Lemon Pickle (South Indian)
(frying method)

Ingredients

18 large lemons   1 tsp turmeric powder
3/4-1 cup salt (as desired)   1 tsp asafoetida powder
2-3 tbsp chilly powder (to taste) 1 tsp fenugreek powder
4-6 tbsp oil   1 tsp mustard seeds

Method

1. Wash, wipe and cut 12 lemons into very small pieces discarding the seeds. Extract juice of 6 lemons and set aside. Cut the peel if soft and fresh, and add to the rest of the pieces.

2. Heat the oil, add the mustard and when done, the lemon pieces and turmeric powder. Stir fry on low heat until the pieces become soft.

3. Add the chilly, fenugreek and asafoetida powders, and continue to fry adding salt.

4. When sufficiently done (the oil stands on the surface), add the lemon juice and mix thoroughly.

5. Remove from fire, cool and bottle.

Note

If desired a few pieces of cut green chillies and slivered ginger can also be added and sauted (in step 2) before adding the rest of the ingredients. In this case reduce the chilly powder.

Instead of adding the masala powders, you could fry 12-15 red chillies, a piece of asafoetida, and one teaspoon of fenugreek seeds in 2 teaspoonsful of oil, then cool and powder. Add this prepared powder along with the lemon juice in step 4. Since the powder is freshly prepared the pickle will taste better.

Lemon Thokku (Tamil Nadu)

Ingredients

6 lemons
2-3 tsp chilly powder (or to taste)
1 tbsp salt (or to taste)
a small piece of asafoetida
1/2 tsp turmeric powder
1/2 tsp mustard seeds
2 tbsp sesame seed oil
2 sprigs curry leaves

Method

1. Wash, wipe and chop the lemons, and remove the seeds. Add the salt and turmeric powder. Mix and leave in a jar for two days.

2. On the third day, remove pieces from jar and grind to a paste.

3. Heat 1 teaspoon of oil in a kadai, fry the asafoetida, and add the fenugreek seeds. Remove, cool, powder, and set aside.

4. To the same kadai, add the rest of the oil, then the mustard and when done, add the curry leaves along with the ground lemon pulp.

5. Add the turmeric and chilly powders, and continue to fry on low heat until the oil surfaces. Add the prepared powder, mix, and remove from fire.

6. Cool and bottle. It will keep over 6 months.

Lemon Pickle with Green Spices (North Indian)

Ingredients

12-15 lemons	1 tsp turmeric powder
2" piece ginger	2 tsp mustard powder
6-8 cloves garlic (optional)	1 tbsp chilly powder (optional)
12-15 green chillies	1/4 cup sugar
1/2 cup oil	3-4 tbsp salt
1/2 tsp cumin seeds	
1/2 cup vinegar	

Method

1. Wash, wipe and cut the lemons into 4 or 8 pieces, add the salt and turmeric powder, and mix. Leave the pieces in a jar and **sun** for 2-3 days shaking the jar every day.

2. Heat the oil, add the cumin seeds and when done, add the green chillies, ginger and garlic, and saute for 2-3 minutes.

3. Add all the powders, and stir for a while.

4. Add the sugar and vinegar, and simmer for 2-3 minutes. Remove from fire and cool.

5. When sufficiently cool, add the lemon pieces, mix thoroughly, and bottle. Use after 2-3 days.

Lemon Pickle (North Indian)

Ingredients

25 lemons	2 tbsp mustard
1/2 head garlic (optional)	1 tsp fenugreek seeds
25 dried red chillies	1/2 tsp turmeric powder
1 tbsp onion seeds	1 1/2 cups oil
1 tbsp cumin seeds	6 tbsp salt

Method

1. Extract the juice from 12 lemons, add a pinch of salt and set aside.

2. Boil some water. Add a pinch of turmeric powder, add the rest of the lemons, and boil for two minutes Remove the lemons from the water. Wipe with a cloth and allow to cool.

3. Dry roast the mustard, fenugreek, onion and cumin seeds. Roast the chillies with a teaspoon of oil, pound all these along with the garlic into a rough powder and set aside.

4. Cut the lemons into fours. Mix the masala powder with some oil and add the salt, making it into a dough. Stuff the lemons with this and put the stuffed lemons into a jar. If any masala remains, put it in as well.

5. Heat and cool the oil. Pour into the jar along with the lemon juice. Keep the mouth of the jar covered with a piece of cloth.

Sweet and Sour Lemon Pickle (Anglo-Indian)

Ingredients

8 large lemons	1/2 tbsp chilly powder
1 cup sugar	2 cloves
1 cup water	1" piece cinnamon
1/2 cup vinegar	1 1/2-2 tbsp salt

Method

1. Wash, wipe dry and cut the lemons into long thin slices.

2. In a thick-bottomed saucepan, pour half a cup of water, add the whole spices, salt and vinegar, and set to boil.

3. When it starts to boil, add the lemon pieces and cook until they turn soft. Remove from fire, and allow to cool.

4. To the sugar add half a cup of water and boil until a thick syrup is formed. Add the chilly powder, mix thoroughly, remove from fire, and cool.

5. Pour the cooled syrup into the cooled lemon pieces, and mix thoroughly once again. Cool and bottle.

Seasoned Lime Pickle (Anglo-Indian)

Ingredients

12 limes (large)	1 tbsp mustard seeds
10 cloves garlic	1 tbsp chilly powder (optional)
1 1/2" piece ginger	1 tsp turmeric powder
12-15 green chillies	1/2 tbsp cumin seeds
1 cup vinegar	1/2 tsp asafoetida powder
1/2 cup sugar	1 1/2-2 tbsp salt (to taste)
1/2-3/4 cup oil	

Method

1. Wash, wipe dry and cut the limes into eight pieces each. Put the pieces in a jar, add salt and turmeric powder, and set aside for two to three days.

2. Wash the green chillies, scrape the ginger and peel the garlic. Dab with a piece of clean cloth to remove all the water. They should be absolutely dry. Chop all three and set aside.

3. Heat the oil, add the chopped ingredients, and saute for 2-3 minutes until they turn soft without getting browned. Add the powdered masalas one at a time, frying all the while.

4. Add the lime pieces, vinegar and sugar, and mix. Allow to cook for one to two minutes. Remove from fire.

5. Cool thoroughly and bottle.

Lemon Pickle (Sindhi Style)

Ingredients

12 lemons	1/2-1 tbsp chilly powder
juice of 6 lemons	1 tsp turmeric powder
12-15 green chillies	1/2 tsp asafoetida powder
1" piece ginger	2 tbsp salt (or to taste)

Method

1. Wash, wipe dry and slit each lemon into fours, without breaking it at the centre.

2. Mix together all the powdered ingredients with some of the lemon juice, stuff the lemons with this, and put them in a clean jar.

3. Scrape, wash, dry the ginger thoroughly, and cut into slivers. Wash, wipe dry and cut the chillies into thin strips. Add these to the lemons in the jar and pour over the rest of the lemon juice. Cover the jar.

4. Keep the jar in the sun for a couple of days until the pieces have become soft.

Lemon Barley

Ingredients

1 kg lemon juice   12 gm barley powder
1.4 kg sugar   2 tsp lemon essence
1.6 kg water   3/4 tsp KMS (a preservative)

Method

1. Ensure that you have a sufficient number of lemons to yield 1 kg of lemon juice. Wash the lemons, cut and extract the juice. Measure the juice and take the rest of the ingredients in suitable proportions.

2. Mix the barley powder with cold water to a paste.

3. Heat the rest of the water, and when slightly warm add the barley paste gradually, and continue to boil for 1-2 minutes.

4. Now add the sugar, 3 tablespoons of lemon juice, and boil on slow heat until the sugar gets dissolved. When the sugar has fully dissolved, remove from fire, filter (to remove the scum) and allow to cool.

5. When the syrup is thoroughly cooled, add the rest of the lemon juice along with the essence.

6. Mix the preservative with some water, add to the lemon barley, and bottle.

Note   Orange Barley can be prepared in a similar way.

MANGO

1. **Avakkai (Andhra Pradesh)**
2. **Sweet Hot Avakkai (Andhra Pradesh)**
3. **Magai (Andhra Pradesh)**
4. **Vadumangai (Tamil Nadu and Kerala)**
5. **Venthiummangai (Tamil Nadu)**
6. **Mangai Thokku (Tamil Nadu)**
7. **Mango Pickle (West Bengal)**
8. **Mango Pickle (Bihar)**
9. **Sweet Hot Mango Pickle (Uttar Pradesh)**
10. **Sweet Hot Mango Chutney (Punjab)**
11. **Mango Pickle (with Green Masala)**
12. **Spicy Mango Pickle (Coorg-Karnataka)**
13. **Mango Ginger Pickle (Maharashtra)**
14. **Mango Pickle (Gujarat)**
15. **Chundo (Gujarat)**
16. **Sliced Mango Pickle (Karnataka)**
17. **Mango Chutney with Vinegar (Anglo-Indian)**
18. **Vinegar Mangoes (Anglo-Indian)**
19. **Mango Raisin Chutney (Anglo-Indian)**
20. **Mango Sauce**
21. **Green Mango Jam**
22. **Mango Mint Sherbet**
23. **Mango Chutney (Easy Method)**
24. **Mango Jaggery Chutney**
25. **Mango Murabba**
26. **Mango Jelly (Raw Mango)**
27. **Green Mango Preserve**
28. **Mango Marmalade (Raw Mango)**
29. **Mango Jam (Fruit)**
30. **Mango Squash (Fruit)**
31. **Mango Panna (Green Mango)**

Avakkai (Andhra Pradesh)

Ingredients

1 kg mangoes (cut pieces)
250-300 gm salt
200 gm chilly powder
100 gm mustard powder
25 gm turmeric powder
50 gm fenugreek seeds (powder 25 gm and whole 25 gm)
a few cloves of peeled garlic (optional)
¾ - 1 Kg. sesame seed oil

Method

1. Wash, wipe dry and cut the mangoes into fairly large pieces - these should weigh 1 kg. Spread the pieces on a clean cloth on a mat (chatai) and **sun** for a couple of hours or until the pieces are dry - there should be no moisture left on them.

2. Take a large stainless steel bowl or plate, put all the prepared powders into it, add enough oil and mix to form a smooth dough - the oil should be just enough to hold all the dry ingredients together.

3. Keep a clean wide-mouthed jar ready at hand. Take a handful of pieces, mix with the masala so as to coat the pieces thoroughly, and put them into the jar. Repeat this process taking a few pieces at a time until all the mango pieces and masala have been used up. Sprinkle any left-over masala on top.

4. Pour the rest of the oil over the mango pieces, shake the jar, cover and leave aside.

5. Check for oil after a few days - if the oil has been used up and the surface looks dry, pour some more oil on top.

Note

You may add the peeled garlic cloves in step 2 along with the rest of the ingredients.

Sweet Hot Avakkai (Andhra Pradesh)

Ingredients

1 kg cut pieces of mangoes
250 gm salt
300 gm jaggery (powdered)
200 gm chilly powder
200 gm mustard powder
50 gm fenugreek seeds
25 gm turmeric powder
sufficient oil to mix masala powders

Method

1. Put the mango pieces, salt and turmeric powder into a jar, and shake thoroughly to mix.

2. Leave the jar aside for 2-3 days, shaking it once daily. By the end of the third day, you will find that the mango pieces have exuded a lot of water (juice).

3. On the third day, remove the pieces onto a steel plate, pour the mango juice into a bowl and **sun** both separately for a couple of days until the juice is reduced to almost half the original quantity. Remove from the sun and cool both thoroughly.

4. Mix the masala powders with enough oil, coat the pieces with this and put them in the jar as in step 2 and 3 of the previous recipe. Set aside the jar.

5. Add one cup of water to the jaggery and boil until the jaggery is dissolved. Remove from fire, strain (to remove grit), and set to boil again until a thick syrup is obtained.

6. Remove the syrup from fire, pour this onto the mango juice and mix. When completely cool add this to the jar, and mix once again thoroughly. Cover tight and store.

Magai (Andhra Pradesh)
(sliced mango pickle)

Ingredients

20-24 medium mangoes
1 tbsp turmeric powder
250 gm salt
1/2 cup fenugreek seeds
250 gm chilly powder
1 small piece asafoetida
2 tsp mustard seeds
4-6 red chillies (whole)
1/4 kg oil

Method

1. Wash, wipe and peel the mangoes, and cut into thin slices. Add salt and turmeric powder, mix, and put into jar. Cover tight and leave aside for 2-3 days, shaking the jar once daily.

2. On the third day, strain the mango water produced in step 1 into a stainless steel basin. Keep the mango pieces and water separately in the sun for a whole day or until the pieces are dried but not tough (hard). By now the water should have reduced to half its original quantity.

3. Dry roast the fenugreek seeds, cool and powder fine - you should have 1 cup of this.

4. To the mango juice add the chilly and fenugreek powders along with the mango pieces. Mix all of them thoroughly.

5. Heat one tablespoon of oil, fry the asafoetida, remove, cool and powder.

6. Heat the rest of the oil, add the mustard and when done, add the whole chillies, remove and cool.

7. Add the cooled oil to the mango pieces along with the asafoetida powder, and mix well. Put into jar, cover with lid and tie a muslin cloth around lid and store.

Vadumangai (Tamil Nadu and Kerala)
(tender mango pickle)

Ingredients

    1 kg mangoes (very small tender mangoes)
    200 gm salt
    1 cup til oil
    100 gm mustard
    1/4 kg red chillies
    1 tsp turmeric powder

Method

1. Wash and wipe the mangoes. Keep them whole. Mix salt, turmeric powder and oil. Add the mangoes, mix all three thoroughly, put into a jar, and keep aside for two to three days.

2. On the third day, you will find that the mangoes have exuded a lot of water. Take out some of this water and using this, grind the mustard and red chillies to a fine paste.

3. Mix the ground paste with the water in the jar, cover the jar with a tight-fitting lid and store. This pickle will keep a year.

Venthiummangai (Tamil Nadu)
(mangoes with fenugreek seeds)

Ingredients

    4 medium mangoes (seeds not yet formed)
    1-1 1/2 tbsp chilly powder (or to taste)
    1 tsp turmeric powder
    1 1/2 tsp fenugreek seeds
    1 small piece of asafoetida
    2 tbsp oil
    2 tbsp salt (or to taste)

Method

1. Wash, wipe dry and cut the mangoes (with their skins) into small pieces, discarding the seeds.

2. In 2 teaspoons of oil fry the asafoetida and fenugreek seeds, powder, and set aside.

3. In a large steel bowl put in the mango pieces, add salt, and mix. Put the turmeric and chilly powders in the centre of the pieces.

4. Heat the oil, add the mustard and when done and while the oil is still hot, pour it over the chilly-turmeric powders. Sprinkle the fenugreek-asafoetida powder and mix thoroughly.

5. Cool and bottle.

Mangai Thokku (Tamil Nadu)
(grated mango chutney)

Ingredients

6 medium mangoes	1 1/2 tsp fenugreek seeds
1/2 cup salt (or to taste)	1 small pinch of asafoetida
2-3 tbsp chilly powder (or to taste)	1/2-3/4 cup oil
1 tsp turmeric powder	1 tsp mustard seeds

Method

1. Wash, wipe dry and grate the mangoes. Add some salt, a pinch of turmeric powder, and set aside.

2. In 1 1/2 teaspoons of oil fry the asafoetida and fenugreek seeds, remove from kadai, powder, and set aside.

3. Squeeze the water from the gratings, and discard the water. Heat the oil, add the mustard seeds and when done add the gratings and turmeric powder. Fry on low heat until the gratings turn soft.

4. Add the rest of the salt and chilly powder, and continue to fry until the oil sur-
    faces.

5. Remove from heat, add the asafoetida and fenugreek powder, and mix thoroughly.
    Cool and bottle.

Note   Refrigerated, it will keep at least six months.

Mango Pickle (West Bengal)

Ingredients	**Mix together (Panchporan)**
6 firm, medium mangoes	1 1/2 tsp aniseeds (saunf)
6-8 red chillies	1 1/2 tsp nigella (kalaunji)
2-3 tbsp jaggery	1 1/2 tsp cumin seeds (jeera)
4-6 tbsp oil	1/2 tsp fenugreek seeds (methi)
(preferably mustard oil)	2 tsp mustard seeds (rai)
a pinch of asafoetida	
3 tbsp salt (or to taste)	

Method

1. Wash, peel and cut the mangoes into thick slices.

2. Heat the oil in a kadai, and add the asafoetida and panchporan. Break the chillies
    into two or three pieces each, and add to kadai. When the spices are done, add the
    mango slices and turmeric powder, and fry on medium heat until they turn soft. If
    desired you can add some chilly powder at this stage.

3. Add the jaggery and salt, and continue to cook on low heat until a chutney consis-
    tency is reached, stirring now and then.

4. Remove from fire, cool and bottle. Refrigerated, it will keep a couple of months.

Mango Pickle (Bihar)

Ingredients	**Broil and powder roughly**
1 kg firm mangoes	2 tbsp each of the following:
1 tbsp turmeric powder	fenugreek seeds (methi)
250 gm salt	mustard seeds (rai)
2 cups or a little more oil	aniseeds (saunf)
(preferably mustard oil)	nigella (kalaunji)
50 dried red chillies	a small piece of asafoetida
(or) 200 gm chilly powder	

Method

1. Wash, wipe dry and cut each mango into 8-10 pieces. Discard the seeds. Sprinkle some salt and turmeric powder, mix thoroughly, put mango pieces into a jar and **sun** for 3-4 days until they get a little soft.

2. Remove water from the pieces by straining. Discard the water and put pieces into a wide-mouthed stainless steel vessel. Set aside.

3. Dry roast the masalas one at a time until done, and remove from kadai. Add 1 tablespoon or so of oil, fry the asafoetida and red chillies, and add to the rest of the masalas. Powder roughly in a mixer-grinder.

4. Mix the masala powder with about a cup of oil, add the mango pieces, and mix thoroughly to coat all the pieces. Put them back in the jar.

5. Pour the rest of the oil on top, cover jar and and keep in the sun for a week or so or until well blended. Check for oil before storing. If not sufficient, add some more at this stage.

Sweet Hot Mango Pickle (Uttar Pradesh)

Ingredients

1 kg firm, raw mangoes
250-300 gm jaggery (to taste)
150-200 gm salt
1 tbsp turmeric powder
2 tbsp mustard seeds
30-50 red chillies
2-3 small pieces of asafoetida
1-1 1/2 cups mustard oil

Method

1. As in the previous recipe, prepare the mango pieces, sunning them.

2. Fry the chillies and asafoetida in a little oil. Cool, then add the mustard seeds and powder. To this, add any left-over turmeric powder and salt. Mix and keep aside.

3. Add some water to the jaggery, and make a syrup of one thread consistency. Remove from fire, and cool.

4. Strain the water from the mangoes. Put them into a large stainless steel vessel. Add the masala powders with about a cup of oil, and coat the mango pieces with this by mixing them.

5. Add the jaggery syrup, mix thoroughly, and put the pieces into a jar.

6. Heat the rest of the oil. Cool thoroughly, pour over pieces in jar, cover and **sun** for a week or so before use.

Sweet Hot Mango Chutney (Punjab)

Ingredients

1 kg mangoes
1/2 cup sugar
4-6 tbsp salt
1 tbsp nigella (kalaunji)
1 tbsp mustard seeds

1 tbsp aniseeds (saunf)
1/2 tbsp peppercorns
25-30 red chillies
1 tsp fenugreek seeds (methi)
a small piece of asafoetida

Method

1. Wash, wipe dry and cut the mangoes into very small pieces, sprinkle salt and sugar, mix well and leave them in the sun for 2-3 days or until the pieces get soft and sticky.

2. Keep all the masalas also in the sun except for the fenugreek and asafoetida. Broil these, add to the rest and powder roughly. If desired half a tablespoon of nigella can be added whole to the prepared powder.

3. Transfer the mango pieces onto a thick-bottomed vessel along with the water that was exuded. Cook on low heat until all the water is absorbed and the pieces are almost dry.

4. Add the prepared powder, mix, cook a further 5-7 minutes or until the masalas are well blended. Remove from fire. Cool and bottle.

Mango Pickle (with Green Masala)

Ingredients

8 medium mangoes
6 tbsp salt or to taste
12 cloves garlic (minced)
1" piece ginger (minced)
15-20 green chillies (slit)
1/2-3/4 cup oil

1 1/2 tsp turmeric powder
1 tbsp chilly powder (optional)
1 1/2 tbsp mustard powder
1/2 tsp asafoetida powder
1 tsp fenugreek powder
1/2 cup vinegar

Method

1. Wash, wipe and cut the mangoes into medium-sized pieces, sprinkle some salt, and leave aside for a few hours.

2. Boil the rest of the salt with some water until a thick solution is formed. Keep aside this brine solution.

3. Heat the oil, add the green chillies, garlic and ginger, and saute for 2-3 minutes. Add all the masala powders, and fry for another one to two minutes. Remove from fire and cool.

4. Strain the mango pieces, discard the water, and put these into a bowl. Add the fried masalas, vinegar, and the prepared brine solution. Mix thoroughly and bottle.

Spicy Mango Pickle (Coorg-Karnataka)

Ingredients

6 medium mangoes (seeds formed)
3/4 cup salt
1 tsp turmeric powder
1 1/2-2 tbsp chilly powder (to taste)
1 small ball of jaggery (powdered)
12 cloves garlic, crushed
1 small piece of ginger, chopped

Seasoning

4 tbsp til oil
1 tsp mustard
3 cloves
2 sprigs curry leaves

Broil and powder

4 tbsp coriander seeds
1 tbsp cumin seeds
1 tsp mustard
1" cinnamon
3 cloves

Method

1. Wash, wipe, clean and deseed the mangoes. Cut into medium-sized pieces, sprinkle salt and turmeric powder, mix well, and set aside.

2. Heat the oil, season with mustard, cloves and curry leaves, add the garlic, ginger and mango pieces (after straining the water out), and fry on very low heat until the pieces get slightly soft.

3. Now add the chilly and jaggery powders, and simmer until blended.

4. Add the prepared masala powder, mix well and continue to cook until the oil surfaces.

5. Remove from fire, cool thoroughly and bottle.

Mango Ginger Pickle (Maharashtra)

Ingredients

1 kg mangoes	150 gm chilly powder
250 gm salt	1 tbsp turmeric powder
100-150 gm ginger	2 tsp mustard seeds
100 gm garlic	2 tsp fenugreek seeds
4 sprigs curry leaves	1/2-3/4 cup oil

Method

1. Wash, wipe and cut the mangoes into 8-10 pieces each. Discard the seeds.

2. Scrape the ginger, wash thoroughly, and wipe dry. Peel the garlic and grind both together to a paste.

3. Heat the oil, add the mustard and fenugreek seeds, and when done add the curry leaves. A large pinch of asafoetida can be added if desired.

4.   Add the ginger-garlic paste, and saute on low heat until the oil surfaces, adding the turmeric and chilly powders while continuing to fry. Add salt, mix thoroughly, remove and cool.

5.   Add the cut mango pieces to the fried masala, and mix thoroughly to coat all the pieces fully.

6.   Put these into a jar, cover mouth of jar with a thin muslin cloth, and set jar in the sun for a week or so until the oil surfaces. If it appears dry add some more oil.

Mango Pickle (Gujarat)

Ingredients

1 kg firm mangoes	2 tbsp mustard seeds
200-250 gm salt	8-10 tbsp chilly powder
1 tbsp turmeric powder	4-5 cloves
2 tbsp fenugreek seeds	1" piece cinnamon
1 large pinch of asafoetida	1-1 1/2 cups oil

Method

1.   Wash, wipe dry and cut the mangoes into 6-8 pieces each. Put them into a large mixing bowl, sprinkle half the salt and turmeric powder, mix well, and set aside.

2.   Broil salt in a kadai on low heat, and remove.

3.   Into the same kadai pour one tablespoon of oil, fry the asafoetida, then the fenugreek seeds to golden brown. Remove, powder, and set aside.

4.   Heat the rest of the oil, add the whole spices (cloves and cinnamon) and when done remove the kadai from fire. Add the chilly powder and salt, mix, and cool.

5.   Strain the mango pieces and discard the water.

6.   Pour the cooled oil over the mango pieces, add the fenugreek-asafoetida powders, and mix thoroughly.

7.   Put the pickle into an earthenware jar, **sun** for 4-5 days, cover and store.

Chundo (Gujarat)
(sweet-hot chutney)

Ingredients

1/2 kg firm, green mangoes
250-300 gm sugar
1 tsp cumin seeds, broiled and powdered
1/2 tbsp chilly powder
1 tsp turmeric powder
salt to taste

Method

1. Wash, wipe dry and grate the mangoes using a medium grater. Sprinkle the salt, sugar and turmeric powder, mix thoroughly and leave in the sun for a whole day or two till the sugar has melted and has formed a syrup. The gratings will be sticky.

2. Remove from the sun, sprinkle the chilly and cumin seed powder, mix thoroughly and bottle.

Note This will keep for a long while. This can be served with bread or rotis.

Sliced Mango Pickle (Karnataka)

Ingredients

6 mangoes
1/2 cup oil
1/2 cup salt
12 green chillies
1/2 tsp turmeric powder
1/2 tbsp chilly powder
1/2 tbsp mustard powder
1 tbsp sugar (optional)

Dry roast and powder

1 tbsp sesame seeds
1/4 tsp asafoetida
1/2 tsp fenugreek seeds

Seasoning

1/2 tsp mustard powder
1 sprig curry leaves

Method

1. Clean and peel the mangoes. Cut into thin slices.

2. Chop the chillies.

3. Season the mustard and curry leaves in hot oil. Add the chopped chillies and mango slices, and fry on low heat until the mangoes turn soft. Add the chilly powder, turmeric and salt and continue to fry until the oil surfaces. At this stage you may add a tablespoon of sugar if the mangoes are too sour. Remove from fire.

4. Add the mustard and masala powders, and mix well.

5. Cool and bottle.

Mango Chutney with Vinegar (Anglo-Indian)

Ingredients

500 gm mangoes	1 1/2 tsp aniseeds
150 gm jaggery	1 1/2 tsp onion seeds
25 gm garlic	10 dried red chillies
25 gm ginger	or 2 tbsp chilly powder
45 gm salt	1 cup vinegar
1 tsp turmeric powder	4 tbsp oil

Method

1. Pound the red chillies coarse using a pestle and mortar. Add the ginger and garlic, and pound along with the chillies. Pound the jaggery separately.

2. Peel and slice the mangoes into small pieces.

3. Season the aniseeds and onion seeds in hot oil. When done, add the pounded ingredients (except the jaggery), turmeric powder and mango slices. Fry for a few minutes until the mangoes turn soft.

4. Add the jaggery, vinegar and salt and stir on low heat until all the slices are cooked and the chutney is thick.

Vinegar Mangoes (Anglo-Indian)

Ingredients   **Grind to a paste in vinegar**

1 kg mangoes   30 gm garlic
3 tbsp sugar   30 gm ginger
120 gm salt   1 1/2 tbsp cumin seeds
1 1/2 cups vinegar   2 tbsp mustard seeds
1 1/2 cups oil   2 tsp pepper
5 sprigs curry leaves   25 dried red chillies
1 tsp turmeric powder

Method

1. Wash, wipe and cut the mangoes into 8 pieces each. Put in a jar and sprinkle half the salt and half of the turmeric powder. Keep the jar in the sun for 1-2 days depending on the heat, stirring the contents occasionally. The pieces must not get very dry.

2. Heat the oil and add the curry leaves, ground masala, the rest of the turmeric powder and fry until the oil surfaces.

3. Remove the mango pieces from the salt water. Add it to the mixture and fry for 3-4 minutes. Now add the salt water, the rest of the salt, vinegar and sugar. Cook on low heat for 15-20 minutes.

4. Remove from heat. Cool and bottle.

Note   A large lump of jaggery may be substituted for sugar.

Mango Raisin Chutney (Anglo-Indian)

Ingredients

1/2 kg mangoes	2 tbsp raisins
1 cup sugar	2 tsp chilly powder
25 gm garlic	1 tsp garam masala powder
25 gm ginger	1/2 tsp pepper powder
60 gm salt	a pinch of turmeric powder
1 cup vinegar	2 tbsp oil

Method

1. Wash, wipe dry, peel and slice the mangoes into very small pieces. Clean the raisins.

2. In 2 tablespoons of vinegar grind the ginger and garlic.

3. Heat the oil, add the ground paste, and saute for 2-3 minutes adding all the powdered masalas.

4. Add the rest of the vinegar, salt, sugar, mango pieces and raisins, and simmer on low heat until a chutney consistency is reached. Remove from fire.

5. Cool thoroughly and bottle. It will keep 3-4 months.

Mango Sauce

Ingredients

12-15 small mangoes (about 1 cup pulp)
1 tsp cumin seeds
1 tsp mustard
3-4 red chillies
a pinch of turmeric powder
2 tbsp oil
1 1/2-2 cups jaggery (depending on the sourness of pulp)
1/2 cup vinegar
salt to taste

Method

1. Boil the mangoes in a lot of water with their skins on until they turn soft. Cool, discard the skins, mash the pulp, remove the fibres, and set aside. This should yield one cup of pulp.

2. Grind the mustard, cumin seeds, red chillies and turmeric in vinegar to a paste.

3. Heat the oil, add the ground masala paste, and stir fry until the oil surfaces. Add the mango pulp, salt, jaggery and simmer until a sauce consistency is reached. Remove from fire, cool and bottle.

Note   Half a teaspoon of garam masala powder may be added in step 3 if desired.

Green Mango Jam

Ingredients

4-5 medium mangoes yielding 1 cup pulp
1 1/2-2 cups sugar (according to the sourness of pulp)
a very tiny pinch of salt and citric acid
1/2 tsp cardamom powder (optional)
a pinch of saffron or 2-3 drops of yellow food colour

Method

1. Peel and slice the mangoes. Add sufficient water to cover pieces, and simmer until the pieces turn soft. Remove from fire, mash thoroughly, and remove fibre if any. The yield should be one cup.

2. To this pulp add the sugar, citric acid and salt, and mix. Simmer until a jam consistency is reached. If you are using saffron add this along with the sugar.

3. Remove pan from fire, add the colour (if you are using this) along with the cardamom powder, and mix thoroughly. Allow to cool and bottle.

Mango Mint Sherbet

Ingredients

3-4 medium mangoes
sugar
a handful of chopped mint
1" piece ginger, thinly sliced
1/2 tsp peppercorns and 1/2 tsp cumin seeds crushed roughly (optional)
a pinch each of citric acid and salt
a few drops of green food colour

Method

1. Wash, peel and slice the mangoes. Add enough water for the slices to immerse. Add the mint, ginger, crushed spices and salt, and boil until the slices are very soft.

2. Remove from fire, mash thoroughly and pass through a sieve to extract the juice. Measure the juice and take an equal quantity of sugar or a little more as desired. Keep the pulp separate for the next recipe.

3. Boil the sugar with 1-1 1/2 cups of water on low heat until the sugar dissolves. Now boil briskly adding salt and citric acid until the syrup forms a one thread consistency. If there is any scum forming, remove from time to time.

4. When the syrup is of a one thread consistency, remove from fire, add food colour, mix and cool thoroughly. Add the juice, mix well, cool and bottle.

Note

To serve, mix the juice with some water, and add a few ice-cubes. It makes a very refreshing drink on a summer day.

Mango Chutney (Easy Method)

Ingredients

mango pulp from the recipe above
2 tbsp refined oil
1 tsp mustard
2 sprigs curry leaves
1-2 tsp chilly powder (to taste)
1/2 tsp turmeric powder
2 tsp sugar
salt to taste

Method

1. After straining the juice for the sherbet, cool the boiled pulp, pass through a mixer, and take out approximately one cup of puree.

2. Heat the oil, add the mustard seeds and when done, the curry leaves. Add the mango puree, turmeric and chilly powders, sugar and salt to taste.

3. Stir fry on very low heat until the oil surfaces. Remove from fire, cool and bottle. Refrigerated, it will keep about a month.

Mango Jaggery Chutney
(without oil)

Ingredients

1/4 kg green medium mangoes, sliced
250-300 gm jaggery (as desired)
a handful of raisins
a large pinch of cinnamon powder
1" piece ginger, minced
3 cloves garlic, minced
2 red chillies (broken) or 1/2 tsp chilly powder
1/2 cup vinegar
salt to taste

Method

1. Wash, peel and slice the mangoes to the desired size. Sprinkle some salt, and leave aside for 4-5 hours.

2. In a thick-bottomed saucepan, mix the vinegar and jaggery. Simmer till the jaggery dissolves. Remove from fire, strain to remove grit, and put back on fire. Strain the mangoes, discard the water, and add to pan.

3. Add all the ingredients, and simmer on low heat until a chutney consistency is reached. Cool and bottle.

Mango Murabba

Ingredients

1 kg mango pieces (peeled and cut)
1 1/2-2 kg sugar (as desired)
1 litre water
1 tsp citric acid
20 gm (about 1 tbsp) chunnam (lime)

Method

1. Prick the mango pieces with a sharp needle.

2. Dissolve the lime in water, and soak pieces in this for 8 hours or overnight.

3. Strain the lime water, and discard; then wash pieces in fresh water 2-3 times. Tie the pieces in a thin muslin cloth, and dip in boiling water for 5-7 minutes. Remove from water, and spread the pieces on a fresh piece of cloth to dry. Weigh the pieces - they should be 1 kg.

4. Dissolve the sugar in water, add the citric acid, and boil for 2-3 minutes. Remove the scum that forms on top. Remove syrup from fire, and strain.

5. Boil the syrup until a one thread consistency is reached. Add the mango pieces, and simmer further for 3-5 minutes or until the pieces are coated with a syrup which will be very sticky. Remove from fire.

6. Cool and bottle.

Note   If desired a large pinch of cardamom powder may be added in step 5.

Mango Jelly (Raw Mango)

Ingredients

> 6 medium mangoes
> 1 tbsp lime juice
> water
> sugar
> a few drops of green food colour

Method

1. Wash, peel and cut the mangoes into slices.

2. Put the mango slices in a thick-bottomed pan, add enough water to cover the pieces, and cook until the pieces are very soft. Remove from fire, and cool.

3. Transfer the pulp to a jelly bag or a thin muslin cloth tied at the top to form a bag. Allow the pulp to drip, overnight if possible.

4. Measure the extract. For every cup of extract, take an equal amount of sugar, and add to the extract along with the lime juice and a pinch of salt.

5. Boil on low heat until the sugar dissolves, then raise the heat and boil until a jelly stage is reached.

6. Remove from fire. Add the colour, mix, and pour into sterilised bottles.

Green Mango Preserve

Ingredients

8-10 small green mangoes (enough to give 1/4 kg when ready)
250-300 gm sugar (to taste)
2 cloves, 2 green cardamoms, 2 one-inch sticks cinnamon
a few drops of green food colour
1 tsp lime (chunnam)

Method

1. Wash, skin, and de-seed the mangoes. Cut them into even-sized pieces and weigh. The pieces should be 1/4 kg in weight. Tie the spices in a spice bag or a thin muslin cloth, and keep aside.

2. Dissolve the lime in plenty of water, soak the pieces (there should be enough water to cover the pieces completely), and leave overnight.

3. Next day, discard all the water and wash the pieces in two or three changes of fresh water. Once again thoroughly drain all the water. Dab each piece with a cloth or paper towel to remove all moisture.

4. Dissolve the sugar in 2 cups of water, add the spice bag and boil until a syrup is formed.

5. Add the mango pieces and boil further until the syrup gets thick and the pieces turn crystal clear (transparent). Since the pieces are to be preserved in sugar syrup, see that there is enough water for syrup while cooking. Also the pieces should be completely immersed in syrup when bottling.

6. Remove from fire, and discard the spice bag (after squeezing it completely). Add the colour, mix thoroughly, cool and bottle.

Mango Marmalade (Raw Mango)

Ingredients

3-4 medium mangoes
1 lemon
sugar
a few drops yellow or green food colour

Method

1. Wash, peel and grate the mangoes. Take out 1/4 kg of gratings, and set aside.

2. Wash and peel the lemon, scrape the inside white portion, and discard. Wash the peel thoroughly and cut into fine shreds. Keep aside 1/2 tablespoon. Extract the lemon juice - take 1 tablespoon, and set aside.

3. Take approximately 250-300 gm sugar (according to the sourness of the fruit).

4. In a thick-bottomed pan put in the gratings, sugar, peel and lemon juice, and simmer on low heat till a jelly stage has reached. Refer to the instructions for making jelly found at the beginning of this book.

5. Remove from fire, add the colour, mix, and pour into sterilised jars.

Mango Jam (Fruit)

Ingredients

1 cup mango pulp
3/4-1 cup sugar (depending on the fruit)
a pinch of citric acid
a few drops of yellow food colour (optional)
a few drops of mango essence (optional)
1 tbsp lime juice

Method

1. Select good, fully ripe mangoes and extract the pulp. Strain the pulp to remove the fibres. If the pulp is not very soft, add some water to the mango pieces and boil to softness.

2. Add the sugar and citric acid to the pulp and cook on a low fire stirring all the while until it reaches jam consistency. Test for setting. (Refer to the instructions for setting found at the beginning of this book.)

3. When set, remove from fire, add the lime juice, colour and essence, and while still hot pour into a sterilised jar.

Mango Squash (Fruit)

Ingredients

>   1 cup ripe mango juice
>   1 cup sugar
>   1 cup water
>   1 tsp citric acid
>   a pinch of Sodium Meta Bisulphate
>   a few drops of yellow food colour (optional)
>   a few drops mango essence (optional)

Method

1. Select firm but ripe fruit. Wash, peel, de-seed and cut into chunks. Add very little water (boiled and cooled) and extract the juice, crushing by hand or using a juice extractor. If it is difficult to extract, then add some water to the mango pieces, boil until soft, cool and then extract the juice. Strain. Measure one cup of juice.

2. Dissolve sugar in 1 cup water, add the citric acid, and boil for one minute. Strain to remove the scum, put back on fire, and boil until a slightly thick syrup is obtained. Cool.

3. When completely cooled, mix the syrup and mango juice. Add the colour and es-
    sence drop by drop until you get the desired colour and flavour.

4. When thoroughly cool, pour into squash bottles.

Mango Panna (Green Mango)
(fresh green mango juice)

Ingredients

1 cup raw mango pulp
2 cups sugar
1 cup water
1/2 tsp citric acid
1/2 tsp cumin seed powder
a few peppercorns
a few mint leaves, crushed
a pinch of green food colour
a pinch of salt

Method

1. Wash, peel and cut the mango into pieces, add enough water to cover the pieces
    and cook until the pieces turn soft. Remove, cool and mash to get one cup of
    pulp. Remove fibre if any. You could roast the mangoes over the gas flame di-
    rectly. When the skin turns dark and crinkly, remove, and cool. Peel the skin and
    mash, discarding the seed and fibres. Get one cup ready thus.

2. Make a sugar syrup with sugar, water, citric acid and crushed mint leaves. Re-
    move the scum as it forms, strain the syrup and cool thoroughly.

3. Broil the pepper and cumin seeds, and powder roughly. Add this powder to the
    cooled syrup. Add the mango pulp and salt, and mix thoroughly.

Note

Serve with crushed ice. It makes an ideal, healthy, summer drink. Please note that this
drink cannot be preserved.

MIXED VEGETABLES/FRUITS

1. **Mixed Vegetable Pickle (Punjab)**

2. **Mixed Vegetable Pickle (Gujarat)**

3. **Mixed Vegetable Pickle (West Bengal)**

4. **Mixed Vegetable Pickle (Tamil Nadu)**

5. **Mixed Vegetable Pickle (Anglo Indian)**

6. **Mixed Vegetable Relish (Western)**

7. **Pickled Vegetables (Western)**

8. **Pickled Vegetables (Chinese)**

9. **Mixed Fruit Jam**

10. **Mixed Fruit Chutney**

The tasty trio: a variety of pickles

The essential 'inputs' needed for achieving luscious 'outputs'

Vital ingredients: the spicy *masalas*

More vital ingredients: savoury dry fruits and other condiments

Mixed Vegetable Pickle (Punjab)

Ingredients

1 medium cauliflower
1/2 kg carrots
1/2 kg turnips (shalgum)
or 1/2 kg knol-kohl
60 gm ginger
60 gm garlic
1 cup vinegar

60 gm mustard powder
60-75 gm chilly powder
120 gm powdered jaggery
1/2 tbsp garam masala, freshly powdered
1-1 1/2 cups oil (preferably mustard oil)
100 gm salt (or to taste)

Method

1. Wash the vegetables. Break the cauliflower into florets, cut the carrots into inch long pieces, peel and cut the turnips into thick slices. If you are using knol-kohl, peel and cut into thick cubes.

2. Tie the vegetables in a clean muslin cloth. Boil some water in a large vessel, immerse the vegetables in it and allow to simmer 3-5 minutes Remove from cloth and spread on a clean thick sheet to allow all the moisture to evaporate.

3. Grind the ginger and garlic in some of the vinegar to a paste.

4. Heat 2-3 tablespoons of oil, add the ground paste and stir fry until the oil surfaces. Remove the pan from the fire. Add the chilly and mustard powder, and the garam masala. Stir for 1-2 minutes and allow to cool.

5. In a large vessel put in the dried vegetables, fried masalas and salt, and add some oil if necessary. Mix thoroughly and put them in a jar. Cover the jar with a clean cloth, tie the cloth at the rim and keep the jar in the sun for 2-3 hours every day for about a week.

6. Soak the jaggery in vinegar and boil to obtain a syrup of a one thread consistency. Cool, pour this into the jar, and mix well, adding the rest of the oil. Make sure that there is a layer of oil on top of the vegetables.

7. Close lid tight and store.

Note

For freshly powdered garam masala use 8-10 cloves, 4 half-inch pieces of cinnamon, 4 large cardamoms, a few peppercorns.

Mixed Vegetable Pickle (Gujarat)

Ingredients

For the pickle masala

150 gm cauliflower
150 gm carrots
30 gm green chillies
30 gm ginger
6 lemons
6 tbsp oil
a pinch of asafoetida
1/2 tsp mustard seeds
1 tsp salt

1/2 cup red chilly powder
1/2 cup mustard powder
1/2 tsp fenugreek powder
1/2 tsp turmeric powder
1/2 tsp asafoetida powder
1 tbsp salt
1 tsp oil

Method

1. Prepare the pickle masala as follows: heat the oil, add the fenugreek powder and asafoetida, and fry. To this, add the rest of the masalas, salt and mix thoroughly. Set aside until needed.

2. Wash and cut the cauliflower and carrots into small pieces along with the ginger. Put these in a vessel. Add water and salt, and set aside for 3-4 hours.

3. Remove the vegetables from the salted water. Wash thoroughly in cold water, then drain and tie the vegetables in a clean muslin cloth.

4. Bring some water in a large saucepan to a boil. Dip the vegetables for 5-7 minutes until they are blanched. Remove from cloth and allow to cool.

5. Extract juice of 4 lemons and cut the others into small pieces. Cut the chillies into small pieces.

6. Heat the oil. Add the mustard seeds and asafoetida and when done, add the chillies. Fry for two minutes and add the lemon pieces. Cook for another minute or two and remove from fire. Add the vegetables, pickle masalas and lemon juice and mix thoroughly.

7. Bottle when cool.

Mixed Vegetable Pickle (West Bengal)

Ingredients

Dry roast and powder coarsely

1 kg fresh vegetables   1 tsp aniseeds (sounf)
(a mixture of cauliflower,   1 tsp onion seeds (kalaunji)
     carrots, and peas)   1 tsp mustard seeds (rai)
2 tbsp mustard powder   1 tsp cumin seeds (jeera)
1 tbsp chilly powder (optional)   1/2 tsp fenugreek seeds (methi)
1 tsp turmeric powder
4-5 red chillies (broken into 2-3 pieces each)
6-8 green chillies (slit)
1 cup mustard oil
salt to taste

Method

1. Wash the vegetables. Cut away the stem of the cauliflower and break into small florets. Cut the carrots into pieces of desired size. Shell the peas.

2. Tie the vegetables in a clean cloth, immerse in boiling water and allow to parboil for three to five minutes.

3. Remove cloth from water, spread the vegetables on a clean sheet and **sun** for a day.

4. Heat the oil, add the green chilllies and when done, the red chillies and roasted powder. (This is called panchporan). Stir fry adding the turmeric and chilly powder along with salt. Cool.

5. Transfer the vegetables onto a large vessel and add the fried and cooled masalas. Mix thoroughly, and put into a jar.

6. Keep the jar in the sun for a few days or until the oil surfaces. If the vegetables are not fully immersed in oil, add some more oil, heated and cooled.

Mixed Vegetable Pickle (Tamil Nadu)

Ingredients

1 kg mixed vegetable
(carrot, cauliflower, beans,
        peas, knol-khol)
8 lemons
a few green chillies (slit)
1/4 cup vinegar
1 cup til oil
4 tbsp salt or to taste

4 tbsp chilly powder
2 tbsp mustard powder
1 tsp turmeric powder
1 1/2 tsp fenugreek powder
1 tsp asafoetida powder
Seasoning
1 tsp mustard seeds
2-3 sprigs curry leaves

Method

1. Wash the vegetables and cut into pieces of the desired size. Shell the peas. Tie them loosely in a thin muslin cloth and immerse in boiling water for 3-5 minutes for them to parboil. Remove from water, and spread on a thick sheet of cloth to dry. Dab them with a paper or cloth towel to remove all moisture.

2. Extract the juice of 6 lemons. Cut the other two into small pieces, and add the pieces to the vegetables.

3. Sprinkle salt, lemon juice and turmeric powder on the vegetables, and set aside.

4. Heat the oil, season with mustard and curry leaves, add the slit chillies, and fry until lightly browned.

5. Lower the heat, and add the masala powders one at a time, stirring all the while.

6. Add the vegetables, and stir fry until they are coated with the masala powders and they become soft.

7. Remove from fire, add the vinegar, and mix well. Cool thoroughly and then transfer them to a jar and **sun** the pickle for a few days.

Note

See that the vegetables are immersed in oil. If not, heat and cool some more oil, and add to jar.

Mixed Vegetable Pickle (Anglo Indian)

Ingredients	Soak in one cup vinegar and grind to a paste
1/2 kg mixed vegetables (cauliflower florets, beans, peas, carrots)	1 tbsp mustard seeds
	1 tsp peppercorns
	2 tsp cumin seeds
8-10 green chillies (slit)	1 stick turmeric
1 cup vinegar	4-6 red chillies (or to taste)
1 cup oil	1 tbsp minced ginger
1-2 tbsp sugar	1/2 tbsp minced garlic
4 tbsp salt or to taste	

Method

1. Wash the vegetables, and drain the water thoroughly. Break the cauliflower into florets, cut the beans into one inch pieces, and the carrots into cubes.

2. Mix the salt with two cups of water. Add the vegetables and keep these overnight in a ceramic jar.

3. Next day drain all the salt water, and spread them on a sheet to dry.

4. Heat the oil, add the green chillies, and when done, add the ground paste and saute on low heat until the oil surfaces.

5. Now add the vegetables, and stir fry for a while. Add sugar, some salt if necessary, and one cup of vinegar. Allow the mixture to simmer for a while, adding additional vinegar if necessary. Remove from fire, cool thoroughly and bottle.

Note

If desired one cup of peeled small red onions (of the Madras variety) can be added along with the green chillies in step 4. Refrigerated this will keep up to three months.

Mixed Vegetable Relish (Western)

Ingredients	**Tie in a spice bag**
1 kg mixed vegetables (cauliflower, carrot, peas,beans, onions and sweet corn)	1 tsp coriander seeds
	1-2 red chillies (cut)
	few peppercorns
1 cup vinegar	1/2" piece cinnamon and
1/2 cup brown sugar	2 cloves roughly powdered
1/3 cup water	1 tsp minced ginger
1/2 tbsp cornflour	
1 level tbsp salt or to taste	

Method

1. Wash the vegetables. Break the cauliflower into small florets, shell the peas, and chop the onions, carrots and beans. Put all of these into a large bowl, add enough water and salt, and leave overnight.

2. Next day drain all the salt water, and spread on a towel or cloth to remove all moisture.

3. In a thick-bottomed pan pour in the vinegar, add the brown sugar and spice bag, and simmer for 15 minutes.

4. Add the vegetables, cook a further 15 minutes on low heat, then raise the heat, and boil for about 5-8 minutes. Remove the bag.

5. Mix the cornflour with water to a paste, add to pan, and cook for another five minutes. Remove from fire, and pour into hot sterilised jars.

Pickled Vegetables (Western)

Ingredients

For the spiced vinegar

1/2 a small vegetable marrow
1/2 a small cucumber
1/2 a small cauliflower
1 medium capsicum
a handful of beans
a handful of shelled peas
a few small onions
salt to taste

2 cups white vinegar
1/2" piece ginger
6 cloves
1/2" piece cinnamon
10-12 peppercorns
3 cloves garlic (optional)

Method

1. Wash and prepare the vegetables thus. Peel and cut the marrow and cucumber into cubes. String the beans and cut into two pieces each, cut the capsicum into one-inch length pieces, and break the cauliflower into small florets. Slice the onions into 2 or 4 pieces each. After cutting, weigh the vegetables separately.

2. Weigh the marrow and cucumber. For every 1/4 kg, use 30 gm salt. In a ceramic dish with a lid, layer the vegetables as follows: put a layer of vegetables, and sprinkle some salt. Repeat this process ending with salt. This method is called *dry brine*. When the layering is over, cover the dish and leave it overnight.

3. The rest of the vegetables should be *wet brined*. For this, weigh the vegetables as described. For every 1/4 kg vegetable, use 30 gm salt dissolved in 1-1 1/2 cups of water. Put the vegetables in a jar and soak them overnight in salt water, ensuring that the vegetables are fully immersed in the brine.

4. Pour the vinegar into a pan, add all the ingredients, and boil for 1-2 minutes. Remove pan from fire, cool and strain. This is the *spiced vinegar*.

5. Next day drain all the salt water from both the dry and wet brine by shaking the vegetables vigorously to remove all the water. Transfer the vegetables to a dry jar or bottle, packing them evenly.

6. Pour the spiced vinegar into the jar one to two inches above the vegetables. Cover tight and store for a few days before use.

Pickled Vegetables (Chinese)

Ingredients

1/2 kg *very fresh* vegetables (as below)	1 cup vinegar
1 small carrot	1 1/2-2 cups water
a small piece of cabbage	1" piece ginger (minced)
a handful of beans	a few cloves garlic (minced)
a handful of spring onions	2 tsp sugar
a few cauliflower florets	a few peppercorns (crushed)
a few green chillies	salt to taste

Method

1. Wash the vegetables thoroughly, and drain all the water. Chop them fine, and put them into a jar.

2. In a pan, pour the vinegar, water and all the ingredients on the right hand side. Set to boil.

3. Simmer for 6-8 minutes, pour over the vegetables in the jar, and mix thoroughly.

4. Allow to cool. Cover the jar and set aside for a few days before use.

Mixed Fruit Jam

Ingredients

1 each (banana, sapota, papaya and guava)
        or any combination you prefer to make 2 cups of pulp
1 1/2-2 cups sugar (depending on the sourness of the fruit)
a pinch of citric acid
colour and essence of your choice

Method

1. Select ripe (but firm) pulpy fruits. Wash thoroughly, wipe clean, and extract the pulp. Soft pulp fruits can be chopped or grated. Hard pulp fruits should be cut into small pieces and boiled with a minimum of water until soft.

2. Put all the ingredients (except the colour and essence) in a thick-bottomed pan and cook the mixture on medium heat, stirring all the while until it reaches jam consistency. Refer to the instructions for making jam at the beginning of this book. Remove from fire when done.

3. Add the colour and essence if desired, and mix well.

4. Fill the jam immediately into hot, sterilised bottles to the brim. Leave the bottles aside until the jam is cooled completely, then seal with wax as given in the instructions for sealing at the beginning of this book. Close lid and store.

Mixed Fruit Chutney

Ingredients

1/2 kg mixed fruits (a combination of fruits like apple, papaya, plums and pears)
1/2 kg sugar or a little more (to taste)
1 medium onion, minced
3 cloves garlic, minced
1/2" piece ginger, minced
a few pieces of garam masala (whole)
1 tsp chilly powder
3/4-1 cup vinegar
salt to taste

Method

1. Wash, wipe and chop or grate fruit, and measure. You should have 1/2 kg. Add one cup of water and boil in a pan until mushy. Add the sugar and mix.

2. Put the minced ingredients along with the whole spices into a spice bag and add the bag to the pan.

3. Cook for a while, then add the salt, chilly powder and vinegar. Cook a while longer until you reach a chutney consistency.

4. Remove from fire and discard bag after squeezing gently to get all the flavour.

5. Pour into sterilised jars. Seal with wax.

ONION

---

1. **Onion Pickle (Tamil Nadu)**

2. **Onion Chutney (Andhra Pradesh)**

3. **Onion Relish**

4. **Pickled Onions (Western)**

Onion Pickle (Tamil Nadu)

Ingredients

1/4 kg small red onions
(Madras variety)
12-15 cloves garlic
1" piece ginger (minced)
6-8 green chillies (slit)
2 sprigs curry leaves
1 small ball of tamarind
6-8 tbsp sesame seed oil

1 tsp mustard seeds
1 tsp turmeric powder
1 tsp chilly powder
1 tsp fenugreek powder
1/2 tsp asafoetida powder
a small piece of jaggery(optional)
salt to taste

Method

1. Peel the onions and garlic, but keep them whole.

2. Boil the tamarind in water and take out extract.

3. Heat the oil, add the mustard and when done, add all the ingredients on the left hand side (except the tamarind). Saute for 5-7 minutes or until the onions are softened.

4. Now add the masalas one at a time, keeping on stirring all the while until the masalas are done.

5. Now add the tamarind extract, salt and jaggery, and simmer the mixture on a low flame until the oil surfaces.

6. Remove from heat, cool and bottle.

Note   Refrigerated, it will keep 2-3 weeks.

Onion Chutney (Andhra Pradesh)

Ingredients	**Seasoning**
4 medium onions	3 tbsp oil
6 dried red chillies	1/2 tsp mustard
1 small piece of tamarind	a large pinch of asafoetida
1 tsp jaggery	2 sprigs curry leaves
salt to taste	1/2 tsp turmeric powder

Method

1. Peel and cut the onions into thick slices.

2. Grind all the ingredients on the left to a rough paste along with the onions.

3. Heat the oil and add the seasonings. Now add the ground mixture and fry on low heat until the oil comes to the surface.

Onion Relish

Ingredients   **A pinch each of the following:**

    1/4 kg small red onions (Madras variety)   chilly powder
    4-6 green chillies, cut into thin circles   sugar
    1/2 cup brown vinegar   pepper powder
    salt to taste

Method

1. Peel the onions, but keep them whole. Put them into a thick bottomed pan, add all the ingredients, and boil for 10-12 minutes or until the onions are tender.

2. Remove, cool thoroughly and bottle.

Pickled Onions (Western)

Ingredients

    1/2 kg small pearl onions
    1 1/2-2 cups white vinegar
    1 tbsp mixed spices (3 cloves, 1 1/2" stick cinnamon, a few peppercorns)
    1 tsp minced ginger
    salt to taste

Method

1. Peel the skin of the onions, wipe, put in a ceramic jar, and sprinkle some salt.

2. Simmer the spices in vinegar for 10-12 minutes. Remove from fire, and cool thoroughly.

3. Pour this spiced vinegar onto the onions so that they are covered fully. Close the jar air tight and set aside for a couple of weeks before using.

ORANGE

1. **Orange Squash**

2. **Orange Marmalade**

Orange Squash

Ingredients

1 cup orange juice
1 1/4 cup sugar
3/4 cup water
3/4 tsp citric acid

a few drops orange food colour
orange essence to taste
a pinch of Sodium Benzoate

Method

1. Choose fresh, juicy oranges. Wash, wipe clean and extract one cup of juice.

2. To the sugar add water, and simmer on low heat for the sugar to dissolve. When fully dissolved, add the citric acid and boil for 1-2 minutes. Remove from fire.

3. Strain the syrup through a muslin cloth immediately. Citric acid removes the scum, and also adds taste to the squash.

4. Cool the syrup thoroughly, add juice, and mix. Add the colour and essence drop by drop until you get the right colour and flavour.

5. Mix Sodium Benzoate in a little boiled and cooled water, and add to the squash.

6. Fill the bottles immediately leaving two to three inches space on top. Cover the bottles and seal with wax.

Orange Marmalade

Ingredients

1/2 kg juicy oranges
2 lemons
6 cups water
3/4-1 kg sugar (according to the sourness of the fruits)
colour (optional)
essence (optional)

Method

1. Wash, wipe clean, and cut the oranges and lemons into halves. Extract the juice. Remove the pips from the fruits, tie in a muslin bag, and set aside both.

2. Scrape the white inside portion of the peel, and take a portion of it. Cut the peel into shreds.

3. In a large bowl put in the 'pip bag', shreds, orange juice and water, and allow it to stand overnight.

4. Next morning transfer the contents into a thick-bottomed pan and simmer gently until the skins of the peels are tender.

5. Remove the 'pip bag', add the sugar, stir to dissolve, and when dissolved completely, raise the heat and boil rapidly until set. When set the marmalade will fall in flakes. Refer to the instructions for making marmalade at the beginning of this book. Be careful not to *overcook* as this will harden the product.

6. While still hot, pour into hot sterilised bottles, and allow to cool before sealing.

PINEAPPLE

1. **Pineapple Jam**

2. **Pineapple Preserve**

3. **Pineapple Chutney (West Bengal)**

Pineapple Jam

Ingredients

1/2 medium-sized pineapple (1 cup pulp)
1 small apple (1 cup pulp)
1 cup sugar
1/4 tsp citric acid
a few drops of yellow food colour
a few drops of pineapple essence
a pinch of Sodium Benzoate

Method

1. Wash, peel and core the pineapple, removing the 'eyes'. Cut the fruit into small pieces. Wash and chop the apples. Put both together in a thick-bottomed pan and boil with very little water until the pieces turn soft.

2. Remove from fire, strain and measure the pulp. Take sugar and citric acid accordingly.

3. Boil the pulp, sugar and citric acid on low heat stirring carefully until it reaches jam consistency. Refer to the hints on jam making at the beginning of this book.

4. Remove from fire, and add the colour drop by drop until you get the required colour. Add the essence to taste. Mix the preservative in a little water and add to the jam, mixing thoroughly.

5. While still hot pour into sterilised bottles, allow to cool completely and seal with melted wax.

Pineapple Preserve

Ingredients

2 cups of cut pieces of pineapple
2 cups sugar
2 each of cloves, cardamom
1/2" piece of cinnamon
a few drops of yellow colour
pineapple essence to taste
a pinch of sodium meta bisulphate

Method

1. Wash, skin, core and cut the pineapple into small pieces. Have 2 cups of these ready at hand.

2. Put the pieces into a thick-bottomed pan, add sufficient water to cover the pieces, add the whole spices and cook on medium heat until the pieces turn tender.

3. Add the sugar and cook further until the pieces appear like crystals and the syrup has the consistency of thick honey.

4. Remove the pan from the fire and discard the spices. Add the colour drop by drop, then the essence, both to your taste. Mix the preservative with a little water, then add and mix.

5. While still hot, pour into sterilised bottles, cool thoroughly and then seal with wax.

Pineapple Chutney (West Bengal)

Ingredients

1 small pineapple
1 tsp turmeric powder
1 tsp chilly powder
2 tbsp sugar
1 tsp flour
3 tsp oil
salt to taste

Mix together (panchporan)

2 tsp aniseeds
2 tsp onion seeds
2 tsp mustard seeds
2 tsp cumin seeds
1/2 tsp fenugreek seeds

Method

1. Clean, core and cut the pineapple into small thin pieces.

2. Heat the oil and add half the quantity of the panchporan. When done, add the pineapple pieces, turmeric, chilly powder, salt, sugar and 2 cups of water. Cook until the pineapple is soft.

3. Mix the maida with some water to a paste and add it to the chutney.

4. Fry the rest of the panchporan on a dry tava. Powder roughly and add to the chutney. Cool and bottle.

Note

Refrigerated, it will keep a few days.

RADISH

> 1. **Radish Tomato Chutney (Anglo-Indian)**
>
> 2. **Radish Pickle (Punjab)**

Radish Tomato Chutney (Anglo-Indian)

Ingredients

1/2 kg radish	3/4 cup sugar
1/2 kg tomatoes	1-1 1/2 cups vinegar
1 tbsp minced ginger	1 tsp cumin seeds
1 tbsp minced garlic	6-8 red chillies
a handful of raisins	salt to taste

Method

1. Wash and grate the radish using a thick grater. Wash and chop the tomatoes. Put them into a thick-bottomed pan.

2. Break the chillies into small pieces, and add to the pan along with the minced ginger and garlic, cumin seeds and salt. Simmer this mixture on a low fire until dry, stirring all the while.

3. Now add the vinegar, sugar and raisins, and boil further until it reaches a chutney consistency. Remove from fire, cool thoroughly and bottle.

Radish Pickle (Punjab)

Ingredients

1 kg radish
125 gm green chillies
4 large lemons
1/2 cup oil
1/2 cup vinegar
30 gm salt

Broil and powder

50 gm mustard seeds
1 tsp fenugreek seeds

Grind to a paste

100 gm ginger
50 gm garlic

Method

1. Scrape and cut the radishes into thin rounds. Cut each round into fours. Cut the chillies into small pieces. Extract juice from the lemons.

2. Fry the chillies in hot oil and add the ground paste. Continue to fry until the oil surfaces. Remove from fire and cool.

3. Mix the radish slices with the salt, fried paste, powdered masalas, lemon juice and vinegar. Place in a jar. Keep the jar in sunlight for 3-4 days by which time the pickle will be ready to eat.

TOMATO

1. Tomato Avakkai (Andhra Pradesh)
2. Tomato Thokku (Andhra Pradesh)
3. Tomato Pickle (Tamil Nadu)
4. Tomato Tamarind Chutney (Tamil Nadu)
5. Tomato Hot Chutney
6. Tomato Spicy Chutney (Anglo-Indian)
7. Tomato Sweet Chutney (Anglo-Indian)
8. Tomato Kasaundi (Bihar)
9. Tomato Green Chilly Chutney
10. Tomato Sauce (Indian)
11. Tomato Sauce (Chinese)
12. Tomato Ketchup (Indian)
13. Tomato Ketchup (Western)
14. Tomato Relish (Western)
15. Green Tomato Apple Chutney (Western)
16. Tomato Preserve
17. Tomato Jam
18. Tomato Jelly

Tomato Avakkai (Andhra Pradesh)

Ingredients

1 kg firm, ripe tomatoes
1-1 1/2 cups sesame seed (til) oil
2 tsp turmeric powder
4 tbsp salt (or to taste)
3-4 tbsp chilly powder

Broil one at a time and powder together

4 tbsp mustard seeds
1/2 tbsp fenugreek seeds
a small piece of asafoetida

Seasoning

2 tsp mustard seeds
2-3 whole red chillies

Method

1. Choose firm, ripe tomatoes. Wash, wipe dry and cut into fours.

2. In a large stainless steel vessel mix together all the dry masalas with some oil to make a soft dough.

3. Keep a clean, dry jar ready at hand. Take a handful of tomato pieces, mix the masala powder coating the pieces, and put them into a jar. Repeat until all the tomatoes are used. If there is any masala powder left, sprinkle on top. Close the mouth of the jar, and leave aside for one to two days. By then the tomatoes would have exuded a lot of water.

4. On the third day, squeeze the pulp separating the water. Keep the tomato pulp and tomato water in two separate wide-mouthed vessels in very hot sunlight for two to three days or until the water is considerably reduced.

5. Heat the oil, add the mustard and red chillies, and when done, remove, and cool thoroughly.

6. Add this seasoning to the tomato pulp along with the tomato water, mix thoroughly and put them back into the jar. Cover and store.

Tomato Thokku (Andhra Pradesh)
(chutney)

Ingredients   **Seasoning**

1 kg firm, ripe tomatoes   1 tsp mustard
12-15 cloves of garlic   1 1/2 tsp urad dal
2" piece ginger   1 1/2 tsp channa dal
6-8 tbsp sesame seed oil   1-2 red chillies
1 tsp turmeric powder   1 tsp cumin seeds
4 tbsp chilly powder (or to taste)
salt to taste   **Broil and powder**
                                      1 tsp fenugreek seeds
                                      a small piece of asafoetida

Method

1. Wash the tomatoes and dip them in boiling water for 5 minutes. Remove, peel the skins, and chop.

2. Add salt to the tomatoes, and set to cook on low heat, stirring frequently until all the water evaporates. Remove from fire.

3. Grind to a paste the ginger and garlic without adding any water.

4. Heat the oil, add the seasonings and when done, the ginger-garlic paste along with the turmeric powder, and fry for a while.

5. Add the chilly powder, salt and tomato pulp, and continue to cook on low heat until the oil surfaces.

6. Add the fenugreek-asafoetida powder, mix thoroughly, remove from fire, cool and bottle.

Tomato Pickle (Tamil Nadu)

Ingredients	**Broil one at a time and powder all together**
1 kg firm, ripe tomatoes	3 tbsp mustard seeds
1 cup sesame seed oil	1/2 tbsp fenugreek seeds
1 tsp turmeric powder	a small piece of asafoetida
4 tbsp chilly powder or to taste	
4 tbsp salt or to taste	
a large pinch of citric acid	

Method

1. Wash, wipe dry and cut the tomatoes into fours.

2. Heat the oil, put in the tomatoes and turmeric powder, and fry until nearly done.

3. Add the chilly powder and salt, and fry for some more time.

4. Add the powdered masalas and mix well, and continue to fry until the oil surfaces.

5. Add the citric acid and mix thoroughly. Remove from fire, cool and bottle.

Note

If you are going to keep this for a long time, add a pinch of Sodium Benzoate after removing from fire.

Tomato Tamarind Chutney (Tamil Nadu)

Ingredients   **Broil and powder**

1 kg firm, ripe tomatoes   1 tsp fenugreek seeds
12-15 cloves of garlic, minced   a small piece of asafoetida
1 1/2" piece ginger, minced
1/2 cup oil (or little more)
1 lemon-sized ball of tamarind
2 tbsp mustard powder
3-4 tbsp chilly powder
1 tsp turmeric powder
4 tbsp salt or to taste

Method

1. Wash, wipe dry and chop the tomatoes. Clean the tamarind removing the pips and seeds, and make into a ball.

2. Heat 2 tablespoons of oil, and add the tomatoes and turmeric powder. Mix. Place the tamarind ball in the middle of the tomatoes and cook all together on a very low flame, stirring occasionally.

3. When the tomatoes are done, remove from fire and allow to cool thoroughly. To this add the garlic and ginger along with the salt and grind to a paste.

4. Heat the oil in a kadai, add the mustard and chilly powders, and saute for a minute. Add the ground paste and stir on very low heat until the chutney is done, at which time the oil will surface.

5. Add the fenugreek-asafoetida powder, mix thoroughly, remove from fire, cool and bottle.

Tomato Hot Chutney

Ingredients

1/2 kg firm, ripe tomatoes
1 tbsp vinegar
a small ball of tamarind
2-3 tbsp chilly powder
1 tsp turmeric powder
1 tsp aniseed powder
1/2 cup oil
2 tbsp salt
a pinch of Sodium Benzoate

Seasoning

1 tsp mustard seeds
1/2 tsp asafoetida powder

Method

1. Wash, wipe dry and cut the tomatoes into medium-size pieces.

2. Clean the tamarind, boil in a little water, extract thick pulp, and set aside.

3. Heat the oil, add the seasonings and when done, add the tomatoes and fry on low heat until nearly done.

4. Add the tamarind extract, all the masala powders along with salt, and simmer on low heat until the oil surfaces.

5. Remove from fire, add the vinegar and Sodium Benzoate, and mix. Cool and bottle.

Tomato Spicy Chutney (Anglo-Indian)

Ingredients

1 kg firm, ripe tomatoes
3 tsp minced ginger
2 tsp minced garlic
a few curry leaves
1 cup oil
1/2-3/4 cup vinegar
1/4 cup sugar
4 tbsp salt or to taste

Soak in vinegar and grind to a paste

1 tbsp mustard
1 tbsp cumin seeds
1/2 tsp fenugreek seeds
15-20 red chillies

Method

1. Wash, wipe dry and chop the tomatoes.

2. Grind the ginger and garlic to a paste.

3. Heat the oil, add the curry leaves and when done, add the ginger-garlic paste. Saute for 1-2 minutes, add the ground masala and fry for a while.

4. Add the tomatoes, sugar, salt and any vinegar left over after grinding. Simmer gently stirring every now and then until a chutney consistency is reached.

5. Remove from fire, cool and bottle.

Tomato Sweet Chutney (Anglo-Indian)

Ingredients

1/2 kg tomatoes
1/2 tsp minced ginger
1/2 tsp minced garlic
1/2 cup vinegar

1-1 1/4 cup sugar
2 tbsp raisins
1/2 tsp garam masala
a pinch of salt

Method

1. Wash, wipe dry and cut the tomatoes into fours. Pick and clean the raisins.

2. In a thick-bottomed vessel, put in the tomato pieces, minced ginger, and garlic, along with the sugar, vinegar and salt. Set to boil on low heat.

3. When half done add the raisins, and cook further until a chutney consistency is reached.

4. Add the garam masala powder, and mix well. Simmer for another minute or two.

5. Remove from fire, and cool thoroughly before bottling.

Tomato Kasaundi (Bihar)

Ingredients   **Soak in vinegar and grind to paste**

1 kg tomatoes   <u>50 gm each</u>
2 tsp turmeric powder   cumin seeds
1 cup refined oil   onion seeds
1 cup vinegar   <u>30 gm each</u>
4 tbsp salt or to taste   mustard seeds
                                           fenugreek seeds
                                           red chillies
                                           ginger
                                           garlic

Method

1. Wash, wipe dry the tomatoes and chop them. Scrape the ginger, peel the garlic, and wash and dry both thoroughly before grinding.

2. Heat the oil, add the ground paste and fry on low heat until the oil surfaces.

3. Add the tomatoes and turmeric powder, and fry for a while.

4. Add the salt, the rest of the vinegar (any vinegar left after grinding the masalas) and cook on low heat until thick, and a chutney consistency has been reached.

5. Remove from fire, cool thoroughly and bottle.

Tomato Green Chilly Chutney

Ingredients	Grind in vinegar to a paste
1 kg tomatoes	12 cloves garlic
12-15 green chillies, slit	1" piece ginger
1-2 tbsp chilly powder	2 tbsp cumin seeds
1 tsp turmeric powder	1 1/2 tbsp mustard seeds
1 cup oil	1 tsp fenugreek seeds
1 cup vinegar	a pinch of asafoetida
1/2 cup sugar	
4 tbsp salt	

Method

1. Wash, wipe and cut the tomatoes into fours. Wash and wipe dry the ginger and garlic before grinding.

2. Heat the oil, add the green chillies, and fry for a while. Add the ground paste, and continue to fry until the oil surfaces.

3. Add the tomatoes and fry until they turn soft.

4. Add the chilly powder, salt and sugar, and cook for a few minutes. Add the vinegar and simmer on low heat until a chutney consistency is reached.

5. Remove from fire, cool and bottle.

Tomato Sauce (Indian)

Ingredients

1 kg tomatoes
1 cup sugar
1 1/2 cups vinegar
2 tbsp salt

15 dried red chillies
1" piece ginger
8 cloves garlic

Method

1. Wash and wipe the tomatoes. Cut into fours and leave in a large-mouthed vessel.

2. Grind the chillies, ginger and garlic to a fine paste in half the vinegar. Add this ground masala to the tomatoes and cook until the tomatoes turn soft and the masalas are done. Remove from fire, cool and strain to take out the thick pulp. Discard the skin and seeds.

3. To the cooked pulp, add the salt, sugar and the rest of the vinegar. Simmer the mixture for 20 minutes or so until it is thick. Remove from fire, cool and bottle.

Note   Some vinegar may be added on top in each bottle. This helps to preserve it.

Tomato Sauce (Chinese)

Ingredients

1/2 kg tomatoes
4 garlic cloves
1 medium onion
2 tbsp sugar
2 drops orange colour (optional)
salt to taste

Spices

3 cloves
3 cardamoms
1" cinnamon stick
1/2 tsp cumin seeds
1/2 tsp pepper
1/2 cup vinegar

Method

1. Wash and chop the tomatoes. Mince the onion and garlic.

2. Mix the spices together and tie in a muslin bag.

3. To the chopped tomatoes add the minced garlic, onion and the spice bag and cook until the tomatoes are done.

4. Cool and squeeze all the liquid from the bag. Pass this pulp through a sieve.

5. Add the sugar, salt and vinegar to the liquid and bring the mixture to a boil. Reduce the heat and simmer for some more time stirring constantly. Remove from heat and add the colour.

Tomato Ketchup (Indian)

Ingredients

Tie in a spice bag

Ingredients	Tie in a spice bag
1 kg red and ripe tomatoes	1-2 cloves
2 tbsp sugar	1 large cardamom
1 tsp salt or to taste	1/4" piece cinnamon
1/4 tsp pepper powder	1/4" cumin seeds
1/4 tsp chilly powder	**Add minced**
1 tbsp vinegar	1 medium onion
a few drops red colour (optional)	1/4" piece ginger
	2 cloves garlic

Method

1. Wash the tomatoes, cut into pieces and cook (without adding water) in a thick-bottomed pan until very soft.

2. Remove from fire, and allow to cool. Pass the cooked tomatoes through a strainer to take out thick pulp. Measure the pulp - it should be 2 cups.

3. Put the strained pulp in a pan, add the spice bag, salt and 1 tablespoon of sugar. Cook until the quantity is reduced to half.

4. Remove the spice bag and squeeze to get all the flavour. Discard the bag. Add the rest of the sugar and the chilly and pepper powders. Cook further until a thick ketchup consistency is reached. Test by dropping half a teaspoon on a saucer. If it does not spread then it is done.

5. Add the colour drop by drop until you get the correct shade (optional).

6. Cool, add the vinegar and preservative, and mix thoroughly. While still hot fill hot, sterilised bottles leaving a head space of two inches. Cork and seal immediately.

Tomato Ketchup (Western)

Ingredients   **Boil in one cup of vinegar**

1 kg ripe tomatoes   1 clove
1 medium apple   1 large cardamom
1 small onion   1/2" stick cinnamon
2 tbsp sugar or to taste   1/4 tsp cumin seeds
2 tsp salt (or to taste)   1/4 tsp peppercorns

Method

1. Boil the spices in vinegar for 10-15 minutes Cool, strain, and set aside.

2. Wash, wipe dry and chop the tomatoes, apple and onion, and set to boil in a thick-bottomed saucepan stirring all the while until you get a thick pulp. Remove from fire.

3. Pass the cooked tomatoes through a strainer, and take out as much pulp as you can. If there is not enough pulp the ketchup will be watery.

4. To the pulp add the sugar, salt and chilly powder, and the spiced vinegar. Simmer until you get a thick chutney consistency, then remove from fire.

5. While still hot, pour into hot, sterilised jars. Cork and seal with hot wax.

Tomato Relish (Western)

Ingredients   **Tie in a spice bag**

1/2 kg just ripe tomatoes   2 cloves
1 large capsicum   1/2" piece cinnamon
2 medium onions   1 large cardamom
1 cup vinegar   1 red chilly (broken)
1 cup brown sugar   1/2 tsp mustard
1 tbsp raisins   1/2 tsp peppercorns
2 tsp salt (or to taste)   1/2 tsp minced ginger
                                    2 minced garlic cloves

Method

1. Wash, wipe dry and chop the vegatables. Put them into a thick-bottomed pan.

2. To the pan, add the spice bag, half of the vinegar and salt, and simmer on low heat until a sauce consistency is reached.

3. Remove from fire, take out the spice bag, and squeeze to get all the flavours. Discard the bag.

4. Put the pan back on the fire, add the sugar, the rest of the vinegar and the raisins. Simmer gently until a chutney consistency is reached.

5. Remove from fire, and pour into sterilised jars. While still hot, cover and seal.

Green Tomato Apple Chutney (Western)

Ingredients   **Tie in a spice bag**

1/2 kg green tomatoes   1 clove
1 large apple   1/2" piece cinnamon
2 medium onions   1 cardamom
1 cup sugar   a pinch of pepper and cumin seeds
1/2 cup vinegar
1/4 tsp salt (or to taste)

Method

1. Wash, wipe dry and chop the tomatoes, apples and onions.

2. Put the onions into a thick-bottomed pan with some vinegar and simmer until the onions have turned soft.

3. To the pan add the tomatoes, apple, spice bag, and the rest of the vinegar. Simmer gently stirring constantly so that it does not burn.

4. When the tomatoes and apple are done add salt and sugar, and cook further until a chutney consistency is reached.

5. Remove the spice bag, and press on its side to get all the flavour. Discard the bag.

6. While still hot, pour the chutney into hot sterilised jars, cover and seal.

Note   The same chutney can be prepared with ripe tomatoes.

Tomato Preserve

Ingredients

> 1/2 kg small red tomatoes
> juice of 1 lemon
> 1 cup sugar
> 1/4 cup water
> a pinch of powdered ginger

Method

1. Wash, wipe dry and cut the tomatoes into fours. Set aside.

2. Boil the water, add the sugar and ginger, and simmer on low heat until the sugar has dissolved.

3. Add the tomatoes and lemon juice to the sugar syrup, and cook slowly until the tomatoes have turned soft and have set.

4. Remove from fire and while still hot, pour into sterilised bottles and seal.

Tomato Jam

Ingredients

1/2 kg firm tomatoes
1/2 kg sugar
2 tbsp lime juice
a pinch of dry ginger powder

Method

1. Wash, wipe dry the tomatoes, and cut into fours. Sprinkle the sugar, cover, and leave overnight.

2. On the next day put the tomatoes along with the juice into a thick-bottomed pan and set to boil on gentle heat until the tomatoes are cooked.

3. Add the lime juice and ginger powder, raise the heat and cook until a jam consistency is reached. Test for setting. (Refer to the hints on jam making in the introduction at the beginning of this book.)

4. When done, remove from fire, pour into hot sterilised jars and seal.

Tomato Jelly

Ingredients

    tomatoes
    lemon
    sugar
    water

Method

1. Wash the tomatoes, cut them into pieces, place in a pan and cook gently until soft. Remove and cool.

2. Strain the cooled tomatoes through a jelly bag and measure the liquid.

3. For every two cups of jelly liquid, take 1/2 kg sugar and juice of one large lemon.

4. Put all these into a pan and boil rapidly until set. Test for setting. Refer to the hints on setting to be found at the beginning of this book. Remove pan from fire and while still hot, pour the jelly into sterilised jars and seal.

MISCELLANEOUS

1. **Bamboo Shoot Pickle**

2. **Cauliflower Pickle**

3. **Crystallised Figs**

4. **Pickled Green Peppercorns (Tamil Nadu)**

5. **Peta Murabba (North Indian)**

Bamboo Shoot Pickle

Ingredients	**Grind in vinegar to a paste**
1/2 kg tender bamboo shoots	1" piece ginger
2 sprigs curry leaves	10-12 cloves garlic
3/4-1 cup vinegar	2 tsp cumin seeds
1 1/2-2 tbsp salt (or to taste)	4 tsp mustard seeds
a large pinch of sugar	1 small piece turmeric
4 tbsp oil	6-8 dried red chillies

Method

1. Remove the outer sheets of the shoots with a sharp knife; and cut the tender portions into pieces of the desired size. Scrape off thinly any green portion on the shoots.

2. Soak the cut pieces in sufficient water for a whole day. Next day, drain all the water, add fresh water (enough to cover the shoots), and salt, and cook until shoots are tender. Remove from fire, drain all the water, and set shoots aside. Note that the shoots may be cooked a couple of times more in fresh water in case the bitterness persists.

3. Soak all the dry masalas in half a cup of vinegar. When soft grind to a paste with the ginger and garlic.

4. Heat the oil, add the curry leaves and ground masala, and stir fry until the oil surfaces.

5. Add the bamboo shoots, saute for 3-5 minutes, then add a little salt (if necessary), sugar, and any left-over vinegar. Cook until the oil surfaces.

Cauliflower Pickle

Ingredients

1 medium cauliflower	1 tbsp mustard seeds
1" piece ginger	1 tbsp cumin seeds
4 large lemons	10-12 dried red chillies
2 1/2-3 cups water	1/2 tsp turmeric powder
4 tsp salt or to taste	a large pinch of asafoetida
	a few peppercorns

Method

1. Wash and clean the cauliflower. Break into small florets; chop the stem and thick portions.

2. Wash, scrape and cut the ginger into slivers.

3. Cut two lemons into pieces and extract juice of the other two lemons. Keep aside.

4. Boil the water with salt, and cool thoroughly. To this add the cauliflower florets and stems along with the ginger and lemon pieces. Cover and leave overnight.

5. Next day drain out all the water, and set aside the cauliflower, ginger and lemon pieces.

6. To the drained salt solution, add the dry masalas and grind to a paste.

7. To this paste add the vegetable pieces and mix thoroughly, adding the lemon juice.

8. Transfer them to a jar, cover and store. Refrigerated, this pickle will keep for a week or so.

Crystallised Figs

Ingredients

    figs (not ripe)
    sugar
    water

Method

1. Wash and cut the figs into halves.

2. Cover the fruit with sufficient water, and cook until they turn soft.

3. Strain the liquid, remove fruit, and set aside. Measure the liquid. For every cup of liquid use 4 cups of sugar. Boil this until a thick syrup is formed.

4. Pour the sugar syrup over the fruit, and leave overnight.

5. Next day, boil the figs in the syrup until the syrup gets very thick and transparent. Remove from fire and leave aside for two days. By this time the syrup will have been fully absorbed by the fruit and will have become transparent.

6. Take out the figs and roll in sugar if necessary. Bottle.

Pickled Green Peppercorns (Tamil Nadu)

Ingredients

1 kg fresh green peppercorns
a large piece of ginger
6 large lemons
1/2 tsp turmeric powder
a generous pinch of asafoetida
1/4 kg salt or to taste

Method

1. Wash, pick and clean the peppers. You can retain some of these on the stalk. Wash and scrape the ginger, then cut into slivers. Extract the juice of 4 lemons, cut the other two into pieces, and put all these into a jar.

2. Boil the salt with two cups of water along with the turmeric powder. Cool thoroughly. Pour into jar and mix well, adding the asafoetida powder.

3. Cover the mouth of the jar, and leave aside for a couple of days before using. This pickle will keep for a long while.

Peta Murabba (North Indian)
(ash-gourd preserve)

Ingredients

1 kg blanched ash-gourd pieces	1 tsp citric acid
1 1/2 kg sugar	a few drops rose essence
	or a generous pinch of cardamom powder

Method

1. Select a firm piece of ash-gourd. Peel, then remove the seeds and centre portion. Cut into medium-size pieces. Prick each piece with a sharp needle.

2. To 1 litre of water add 20 gm of lime (chunnam), and mix thoroughly. Add the peta pieces (there should be enough water to cover the pieces) and leave aside overnight.

3. Next day, remove the pieces from the chunnam water (they will have become a little soft). Wash thoroughly two or three times in fresh water, tie the pieces in a muslin cloth, and blanch (dip in boiling water) for 15 minutes.

4. Remove from hot water, spread on a cloth to cool and to remove moisture. Now weigh the pieces and take the rest of the ingredients accordingly.

5. Mix sugar, water and citric acid. Set to boil - 2 parts sugar to 3 parts water. Remove the scum from time to time.

6. When the syrup is clear, remove from fire, and strain through a thick cloth.

7. Put the syrup back on fire, add the peta pieces and cook until you get a 2-3 thread consistency.

8. Remove from fire, cover, and allow to stand overnight.

9. Next day drain off the syrup by straining through a stainless steel sieve. Add the essence or cardamom powder, and mix.

10. Put the pieces in a clean jar, cover, and store.

GLOSSARY

English	Bengali	Gujarati	Hindi	Kannada
Aniseeds	Mowri	Saunf	Sounf	Sompu
Asafoetida	Hingh	Hingh	Hingh	Hingu
Bay leaf	Tejpatta	Tejpatta	Tejpatta	Biryani ele
Bengal gram dal	Cholar dal	Channa	Channe ki dal	Kadale bele
Black gram dal	Kolai dal	Udad ni dal	Urad dal	Uddine bele
Caraway seeds			Shahjeera	
Cardamom	Elaichi	Elaichi	Elaychi	Yelakki
Cashewnut	Kaju	Kaju	Kaju	Godambi
Coriander leaves	Dhanesag	Kothmer	Hara dhania	Kothamiri soppu
Coriander seeds	Dhane	Dhana	Dhania	Kothambari beeja
Cumin seeds	Jeera	Jeera	Zira	Jeerage
Curry leaves	Bursunga	Mithe Limbdo	Mita neem	Karibevina soppu
Fenugreek seeds	Methi	Meethi	Methi	Menthya
Garlic	Lasoon	Lasan	Lasoon	Bellulli
Ginger	Ade	Adhu	Adrak	Hasi sonti
Green chilly	Kamba Launka	Lila mircha	Hari mirchi	Menesinekai
Jaggery	Gur	Gur	Gur	Bella
Mint	Pudeena sag	Fudina	Pudina	Podeena soppu
Mustard seeds	Sharse	Rai	Rai	Sasve
Nutmeg	Jaiphal		Jaiphal	Jathikai
Onion seeds	Kalajeera		Kali jeera	
Peppercorn	Gol mirch	Kali mari	Kali mirch	Karimensu
Poppy seeds	Posto	Khus khus	Khus khus	Gas-gase
Raisin	Kismis	Draksh	Kismis	Drakshee
Red chilly	Sukha lauki	Sukvele mircha	Lal mirchi	Vonamenesinakayi
Saffron			Kesar	Kesari
Sesame seeds	Til	Til	Til	Ellu
Turmeric	Halud	Halad	Haldi	Arshana
Tamarind	Tentul	Amli	Imli	Hunusehannu

GLOSSARY

Malayalam	Marathi	Oriya	Tamil	Telugu
Perinjeerakam	Badishep	Paru kakharu	Perunjeeragam	Perijeerakam
Kayam	Hing		Perungayam	Hinguva
	Tejpatta	Tej patta	Brinji ilai	Biryani akku
Kadala paruppu	Hurbura	Buta	Kadalai parappu	Sanage pappu
Uzhunnu	Udad dal	Bada Kalara biri	Ulatham paruppu	Minappu
Elathari	Velchi	Alaichi	Yelakkai	Elakkayi
Parangiyandi	Kaju		Mundhiri Parappu	Jeedi pappu
Kothamalli	Kothmir	Dhania	Pachai Kothamalai	Kotthimiri
Kothamalli	Dhana	Dania	Kothamalli vidhai	Dhaniyalu
Jerrakam	Jhere	Jira	Jeeragam	Jeera kara
Kariveppila	Kadi limb	Brusunga patra	Kariveppilai	Karivepaku
Uluka	Methi	Methi	Venthayam	Menthulu
Vella mulla	Lasoon	Rasuna	Ulli poondu	Velulli
Inji	Ale	Ada	Inji	Allam
Pache milakai		Kancha launka	Pacchai milagai	Pachimirapakayi
Sarakara	Gur		Vellam	Bellam
Mootha	Pudina	Pudana patre	Pudeena	Pothina
Kaduku	Moheri	Sorisa	Kadugu	Avalu
			Jathikai	
		Kala jeera	Karunjeeragam	
Kurumolegu	Mire	Gol marcha	Milagu	Hiriyalu
Khasa khasa	Khus khus		Khasa khasa	Gasa gasalu
Unnaka munthringa	Manuka	Kismis	Draksha pazam	Kisi misu
Kappal mulaku	Mirchi lal	Sukhila lauka	Milagai vattal	Endi miripikayi
			Kunkuma poo	
Ellu	Til		Ellu	Nuvvulu
Manjal	Halad atta	Haladi	Manjal	Pasupu
Puli	Chincha	Tentuli	Puli	Chintha pandu

INDEX OF RECIPES

—V—